THE LIGHT RAILWAY
A JOURNEY ALONG THE NARROW AND BUCOLIC

Dedication

For Kathryn, Krystal, Richard, Luna, Oscar and Jakob.

THE LIGHT RAILWAY

A JOURNEY ALONG THE NARROW AND BUCOLIC

JOHN SCOTT-MORGAN

AN IMPRINT OF PEN & SWORD BOOKS LTD.
YORKSHIRE – PHILADELPHIA

First published in Great Britain in 2025 by
Pen and Sword Transport
An imprint of
Pen & Sword Books Ltd.
Yorkshire - Philadelphia

Copyright © John Scott-Morgan, 2025

ISBN 978 1 03610 661 4

The right of John Scott-Morgan to be identified as author of this work has been asserted by him in accordance with the Copyright, Designs and Patents Act 1988.

A CIP catalogue record for this book is available from the British Library.

All rights reserved. No part of this book may be reproduced or transmitted in any form or by any means, electronic or mechanical including photocopying, recording or by any information storage and retrieval system, without permission from the Publisher in writing.

Typeset by SJmagic DESIGN SERVICES, India.
Printed and bound in India by Replika Press Pvt. Ltd.

Pen & Sword Books Ltd. incorporates the imprints of Pen & Sword Books: After the Battle, Archaeology, Atlas, Aviation, Battleground, Discovery, Family History, History, Maritime, Military, Politics, Select, Transport, True Crime, Fiction, Frontline Books, Leo Cooper, Praetorian Press, Seaforth Publishing, Wharncliffe and White Owl.

For a complete list of Pen & Sword titles please contact

PEN & SWORD BOOKS LIMITED
George House, Beevor Street, Off Pontefract Road, Hoyle Mill, Barnsley,
South Yorkshire, England, S71 1HN.
E-mail: enquiries@pen-and-sword.co.uk
Website: www.pen-and-sword.co.uk

or

PEN AND SWORD BOOKS
1950 Lawrence Rd, Havertown, PA 19083, USA
E-mail: uspen-and-sword@casematepublishers.com
Website: www.penandswordbooks.com

Contents

Acknowledgements	6
Introduction	7
The Channel Islands	11
The West Country	15
South East England	36
East Anglia	64
The Welsh Borders and Midlands	81
The North and North East of England	105
Wales	138
Scotland	171
Ireland	174
The Isle of Man	221

Acknowledgements

I should like to thank the following people and archives, for their kind help in compiling this book, Richard Stumpf, Derick Sprange, Tom Middlemass, Graham Stacey, Rail Archive Stephenson, Photomatic, Hopwood Collection, Ken Nunn, J.H. Aston, J.G. Dewing, K.A. Stone, D. Stucky, S.W. Baker, AW. Croughton, Lens of Sutton Collection, Ivor Gotheridge, F.M. Gates, J.H. Meredith, W. Pooter, R.G. Jarvis, F.A. Wycherley, F. Edmonds, R.E. Tustin, H. Gordon Tidey, T.J. Edgington, Henry Townley, Rev A.W.V. Mace, R.K. Blencowe Collection. I have made every endeavour to contact all photographers and suppliers of pictures used in this book, however if I have left anyone out I apologise, please contact me through the publisher and I will pay the reproduction fee.

I should like to especially thank my good friend, the late Graham Stacey for all his kind help in printing and supplying many of the pictures in this book over the years.

Introduction

Railways as we know them started in the Middle Ages, where they were used in mines to transport extracted ore from the seams and tunnels. This later developed into more sophisticated methods of operation and construction, when wooden rails and basic single blade points gave way to iron rails and iron point work.

The invention and development of the high pressure steam locomotive opened a new and more advanced chapter in railway development from 1804, with the Pen-y-Darren Tram Road in South Wales, developing during the next ninety years into a national network, crossing the whole of Britain and Ireland.

The final chapter in traditional railway development was the passing of the Light Railways Act 1896, which allowed the construction of minor railways serving areas not already covered by the existing main line system. There had been several pieces of legislation passed in Ireland in the 1880s to allow rural lines to be projected and constructed as minor railways, enhancing the existing main line operations, or local railway companies serving a given area. The Light Railways Act 1896 in Britain allowed for railways of a lighter construction, with minimal signalling and often having level crossings with no gates. The 1896 Act was also used to construct and promote urban and city electric tramways (not covered in this volume).

There were restrictions on train speed as the legislation specified that trains should only run at a maximum of 25mph with one locomotive in steam on a single line operation. Most of the railways set up using the 1896 Act were small rural affairs using small locomotives and basic carriage and wagon stock.

There were however two exceptions to this situation, in the form of the group of lines projected by Lt. Col. Holman Fred Stephens and a syndicate of light railway promoters in the North East of England led by Sebastian Meyer, who in both cases formed operations to manage and operate groups of lines. The group of lines managed and operated by Stephens were managed from offices in Salford Terrace, Tonbridge, where all the lines had a small staff looking after their day to day operations, under the watchful eye of Stephens and his assistant W.H. Austen.

A number of light railways were standalone affairs with local management, however there were light railways that were promoted by main line companies, in order to serve rural areas within their local operating district, which allowed the construction of cheaper lines that required less infrastructure.

The light railways in Ireland were of a different nature, mostly constructed to 3ft gauge, with only a few lines constructed to Irish standard 5ft 3in gauge. In many cases, the 3ft gauge lines were promoted to open up remote areas of the country, mostly in the far West, which had suffered from the potato famine. The new lines were used as a means of encouraging the repopulation of often decimated parts of the country, from where many people had emigrated to other parts of the globe as a result of the famine. In order to allow these railways to prosper, a baronial guarantee system was set up, in order to fund the shortfall in annual finances to operate these socially essential lines.

When the Light Railways Act 1896 was passed, the world was a slower, more localised affair, with horse transport on the roads, which was little or no threat to railways, especially the new light railways being promoted. However, within a decade the first motor cars and lorries appeared, which although small and seemingly inefficient vehicles at the time, would prove to be unwanted competition to the small network of rural byways that appeared as a result of the late Victorian light railway legislation.

The First World War had a profound effect on the light railways of both Britain and Ireland, not only in terms of the domestic war effort, but also in its aftermath, with the availability of new and used motor vehicles, especially chassis that could be re-bodied as goods lorries or buses, which put a great strain on the rural lines that had already suffered from the financial setbacks created by the war. In the post war period things started to look increasingly bleak for the once smart new minor lines of the 1890s and 1900s, which had often opened with great fanfare and expectations of success. There were lines where economies were attempted in the early and mid-1920s, with the introduction of petrol rail cars and small internal combustion shunting locomotives, in an attempt to ease the financial burden of railway operation.

The steam locomotive was still the predominant form of motive power and this together with the now aging rolling stock often took its toll on local light railways both here and across the water. Most of the light railways promoted in the first decade of the twentieth century had opened with new rolling stock and motive power; however, by the third and fourth decade of the twentieth century most lines had second- and often third-hand rolling stock and locomotives that had first seen better days on other lines. Gradually the network of rural light railways started to falter and close down as most had not been grouped into any of the big four railway companies in 1923.

The two syndicated groups operated by Stephens and the smaller group in the North of England seemed to muddle through from one year to the next, but the one-off independent minor lines like the Bishops Castle Railway, a failed main line project from the 1860s which had been in receivership for seven decades, were eventually forced to close down in 1935, such was the financial climate by this time.

Many of the main line operators in the pre and post grouping era, promoted and constructed light railways as a way of serving areas that had been left out, during the initial stages of railway promotion and development. These lines included a number of light railways opened by the Great Eastern Railway (GER) in Essex and East Anglia, such as the Wisbeach and Upwell Tramway and the Kelvindon and Tollesbury line, both these lines serving agricultural areas and were dependent on seasonal traffic.

The Southern Railway opened a new light railway to Fawley on the estuary leading out of Southampton Water in 1925, a line that was later developed to serve the extensive oil refinery that was developed in that location, serving the facility until 2016 as well as the military port at Marchwood.

Many of the main line owned and operated light railways closed down during the mid-1930s, including the Southern Railway-owned Lynton & Barnstaple Railway, closed in 1935, and the former North Staffordshire Railway, later London, Midland and Scottish (LMS)-owned Leek & Manifold Light Railway, closed in 1934.

In Ireland, the situation was somewhat different in that after partition in 1922, the lines in the South in the main became part of the newly formed Great Southern Railway, while the lines north of the border in Northern Ireland were either left as independent railways or had in the previous decade become part of the Midland Railways, Northern Counties Committee (NCC), later part of the LMSNCC, or had joint ownership between two or more railway companies, like the County Donegal Railway, which after 1906 had a joint management committee, owned by the Great Northern Railway of Ireland and the Midland NCC, later the LMSNCC.

This situation became even more complicated after the Second World War, when the Irish Free State became a republic and the newly formed Córas Iompair Éireann (CIÉ) took over the railways, buses and trams in the South of Ireland, while the Ulster Transport Authority took over the nationalised railway and bus network in the North. Again, there were joint management responsibilities, including the County Donegal Railway, with its joint ownership now being vested in the Great Northern Railway of Ireland and CIÉ in the Irish Republic.

The situation by 1945 in England was such that the remaining light railways were on their last legs and about to give up the fight against road competition. The election of that year brought in a Labour government, which had firm plans and policy to nationalise key industries, including railways. Strangely enough, the syndicate set up by Stephens still existed, however the British Transport Commission closed the remaining lines still operated by the syndicate after nationalisation in 1948, the Kent & East Sussex Railway closed to passengers in 1954 and freight on the remaining section between Tenterden Town and Robertsbridge in 1961; East Kent Railway closed to passengers in 1948 and freight in sections from 1951 until 1987; and the Shropshire & Montgomeryshire Light Railway closed in 1960 after the army handed the line back to the Western Region. The other smaller syndicates' lines in the North of England were left as independent railways, these being the Derwent Valley Light Railway, the North Sunderland Light Railway and the Easingwold Light Railway, all of which operated as small concerns until they closed, the North Sunderland in 1951, The Easingwold Light Railway in 1957 and the Derwent Valley Light Railway in 1985.

The light railway age was a final attempt to serve all areas of the British Isles and Ireland, with branch lines that connected the whole nation and attempted to bring about change for the better for rural communities where they were promoted. To this extent in the late nineteenth and early twentieth centuries they largely succeeded and it was only the advent of road motor transport that thwarted their efforts in the post-First World War era.

This volume is not designed to be a history of the British and Irish light railway, but a tribute to a brave attempt often against the tide, to provide cheap reliable transport to some of the remotest communities that had been ignored or left behind by the larger main line railways. To this end, those who promoted and constructed these small transport concerns can only be admired and regarded as local heroes for their brave efforts, in a world that changed so much after the First World War.

The Channel Islands

0-4-2 tank locomotive *Calvados*, constructed by Kitson of Leeds in 1872, stands in the station yard at St Helier, on the Jersey Eastern Railway c.1900, with a train of four wheeled carriage compartment stock. There were four Kitson 0-4-2 tank locomotives on the Jersey Eastern Railway. The line was opened in 1873 and constructed in stages from St Helier to Gorey Pier, which was opened in 1891. The standard gauge line closed to all traffic due to road competition in 1929, despite the introduction of two Sentinel steam rail cars in the 1920s to cut operating costs. *Hopwood Collection*

One of the Kitson 0-4-2 tank locomotives arrives with a train of four wheeled carriage stock at La Rocque station in the early 1920s; at that time there was still considerable local and holiday passenger traffic for the line. *Commercial Postcard*

The Jersey Railway was opened in 1870 and was originally standard gauge. However, this was changed to 3ft 6in gauge in 1884. The line ran from St Helier to Corbiere and operated an intense service for locals and tourists in the summer, here we see a 2-4-0 tank locomotive arriving at Saint Aubin station in the late 1890s hauling a train of four wheeled carriage stock. The line suffered from road competition after the First World War, which led to closure in 1936. *Commercial Postcard*

2-4-0 tank locomotive No.4 *St Brelades* constructed by W.G. Bagnall in 1896, poses for a photograph c.1900. These neat looking tank locomotives were the mainstay of the line from the 1880s until closure in 1936, although latterly two Sentinel steam railcars were employed on some passenger services. *Author's Collection*

The West Country

The Liskeard & Looe Railway was opened in 1844 as a horse tram road, serving the Caradon mines with Moorswater, later being extended in 1846 to Cheesewring, opened through to Looe in 1860, running parallel for part of its formation with the Moorswater canal. The company was an independent standard gauge line until 1909, when it was taken over by the Great Western; the line is still part of the national network today, serving the local community. Here we see the newly delivered Andrew Barclay 2-4-0 tank *Lady Margaret*, constructed in 1901, at Looe Station with a train of four wheeled carriage stock, after arriving from Liskeard c.1901. *Author's Collection*

The Plymouth Devonport & South Western Junction Railway was an independent railway linking Bere Alston with Callington. Opened in 1908, it incorporated part of the 4ft gauge East Cornwall Mineral Railway and had running rights to Devon Port over the London and South Western Railway (L&SWR). Here we see Hawthorne Leslie 0-6-0 tank, *A.S. Harris,* hauling a train of former L&SWR four wheeled carriages on a mixed train c.1910, the line was grouped into the Southern Railway in 1923 and is still open to Gunnislake as part of the national network today. *Ken Nunn*

Gunnislake station c.1908 shortly after opening of the line, with *A.S. Harris* on a freight train, posed for an official picture. The station buildings were built of corrugated iron with double awnings, in the far right one can see a Plymouth, Devonport and South Western Junction Railway (PD&SWR) delivery wagon on display for the camera. *PD&SWR Official*

Calstock viaduct is a major feature of the line, constructed between 1904 and 1907, using concrete blocks. The structure dominates the Tamar River and is an outstanding landmark. Here we see a train of two Southern utility vans and a bogie brake carriage headed by two Adams 02 class 0-4-4 tanks c.1955. *J.H. Aston*

The Lynton & Barnstaple Railway was opened in 1898 linking Lynton & Lynmouth with Barnstaple, constructed to 2ft gauge. The railway was taken over by the L&SWR in 1922 and grouped into the Southern Railway in 1923. Here we see a scene at Lynton & Lynmouth station c.1910 with passengers boarding a train for Barnstaple. The locomotive is Manning Wardle 2-6-2 tank *Taw,* constructed in 1897. The line closed in 1935, however there is a project to reconstruct the railway underway, which has already opened a mile and a half of the line and the organisation is purchasing land to continue reopening the line along its original formation. *Author's Collection*

2-4-2 tank locomotive *LYN* was constructed in 1899 by American builders Baldwin of Philadelphia, at the time when British locomotive builders' order books were full and the Lynton & Barnstaple Railway was in need of extra motive power. *LYN* is depicted in the workshop at Pilton works Barnstaple undergoing repairs in early Southern Railway days c.1925. *Author's Collection*

The last locomotive constructed for the line was Manning Wardle tank No.188 *Lew*, in Southern Railway days, which was delivered to the railway in 1925. After the line closed in 1935 *Lew* was sold to a lumber railway in Brazil and was shipped out of Britain along with a large quantity of rail and some carriage underframes for use on the line in Brazil. Here seen at Pilton yard c.1930 coupled to one of the bogie carriages. *J.G. Dewing*

Manning Wardle 2-6-2 tank 760 *Exe* ascends through the Devon countryside on its way to Lynton & Lynmouth with a passenger service c.1934. The passenger trains often had a bogie van in their formation for local goods and parcels traffic, also milk deliveries. *Author's Collection*

The North Devon and Cornwall Junction Railway (N D & C J R) was a latecomer, in that it opened in 1925, the engineer being Lt Col Stephens. The line linked two sections of the Southern Railway, with junctions at Halwill Junction and Torrington. The line served the clay industry and to a lesser extent local agriculture. Here we see Ivatt 2-6-2 tank No.41290 at Meeth station c.1962 with a train consisting of a single Bulleid brake carriage on a local service. The N D & C J R closed to passenger traffic in 1965, but continued to serve the clay industry until 1982. *K.A. Stone*

Ivatt 2-6-2 tank No.41295 arrives at Dunsbear Halt c.1962 with a local service of a single Bulleid bogie carriage; the stations on this line were a mixture of concrete and stone structures and were of a neat simple design. *J.H. Aston*

The Bideford Westward Ho & Appledore was a standard gauge steam tramway operation, that linked Bideford Quay with Appledore in Devon. Opened in 1901, the line had mixed fortunes throughout its existence. The line was a mixture of urban tramway and light railway, operating primarily for the locals and summer tourist traffic. The line closed in 1917 and the locomotives and rolling stock were sold along with the line's other assets, the locomotives being acquired by the government. One of the three Hunslet constructed 2-4-2 tank locomotives heads a single bogie carriage through the streets of Bideford c.1910. *D. Stuky Collection*

A Hunslet 2-4-2 tank and single balcony end carriage steams through the streets of Bideford. Note the fully encased motion in a skirt and the centre buffer arrangement, normally found on narrow gauge or colonial railways, the three locomotives had names, *Grenville*, *Torridge* and *Kingsley*. D. Stuky Collection

A former Bristol & Exeter 2-4-0 tank simmers in the platform at Hemyock station, on the Culm Valley Light Railway, with a mixed train for Tiverton Junction c.1925. As one can see from the picture, the line had a reasonable amount of goods traffic at this time, which continued into the 1960s as did the milk traffic, which survived until the mid-1970s. *D. Stuky Collection*

The Culm Valley Light Railway was opened in 1876 and was operated by the Bristol & Exeter Railway, later the Great Western, connecting Tiverton Junction with Hemyock, its main traffic being milk and agricultural produce. The line was closed to passenger traffic in 1963 but remained open to milk traffic until 1975. The scene at Hemyock in 1960, with a Great Western 1400 tank locomotive shunting in the yard and the single bogie carriage waiting in the platform for the return working to Tiverton Junction. *Author's Collection*

The Weston Clevedon & Portishead Light Railway opened to traffic in 1897 and was extended to Portishead in 1907. This picture shows Sharp Stuart 2-4-0 tank locomotive No.1384, constructed in 1876, formerly a Great Western locomotive, which had worked on the Watlington & Princes Risborough Railway and the Wrington Vale Branch, before sale to the Weston Clevedon & Portishead Railway. 1384 is seen at Portishead station in April 1911, waiting with a train of American Style balcony end bogie carriages, for the road to Weston via Clevedon. *Author's Collection*

Manning Wardle 0-6-0 saddle tank locomotive No.5, purchased new in 1919, simmers in the platform at Clevedon with a train of four wheeled carriage stock c.1935. An unusual feature of No.5 was that it had disc, rather than spoked wheels and a high pitched boiler, giving it a top heavy look. It lasted in service until the line closed in 1940. In the background can be seen the locomotive and carriage sheds; note the big Drewry petrol rail car, on the far right, which was purchased from the Southern Railway in 1934. *Ivor Gotheridge Collection*

Ex LBSCR A1X Terrier No.2 *Portishead*, formally *Gipsyhill*, constructed in 1877, waits in the platform at Weston, with a train of former L&SWR and Metropolitan Railway carriages in 1935. This locomotive was purchased from the Southern Railway in 1925 and in 1940 became Great Western No.5, after the line's closure. *Ivor Gotheridge Collection*

Manning Wardle 0-6-0 saddle tank No.3 *Weston* constructed in 1881, waits in the platform at Portishead, with a train for Weston c.1936. This locomotive was purchased in 1906 and survived in traffic on the line until closure in 1940, the small Drewry rail car on the right was purchased new in 1921, in an attempt to save money on manning and operating, it also survived until the line closed in 1940. *S.W. Baker*

The Axminster and Lyme Regis Light Railway linked the two towns and was promoted locally and by the L&SWR, opening in August 1903, being taken over completely by the L&SWR in 1907. The railway had sharp curves and lightly constructed track in keeping with light railway practice, the only intermediate station being Combpyne, a halt half way along the line. The railway originally used two second hand Brighton Terrier 0-6-0 tank locomotives for its train services, later replaced for a time with 02 class 0-4-4 tanks, which were not very successful, however it was found that the Adams Radial 4-4-2 tanks were ideal for the tortuous sharp curves along the lines formation and lasted in use until 1961, when Ivatt 2-6-2 tanks were briefly used before the Western Region introduced single car DMUs. The line was finally closed as part of the Beeching plan in November 1965; today, the most tangible evidence of the line is Cannington viaduct, here seen during construction in 1902. *D. Sprange Collection*

Lyme Regis station c.1910, with a 02 Class 0-4-4 tank and L&SWR non-corridor bogie carriage stock in the platform. The station building was acquired by the preserved Mid Hants Railway after closure and is now at Arlesford station. *D. Sprange Collection*

Two of the three Adams Radial 4-4-2 tank locomotives, No.30583 leading, haul a summer special service along the line, consisting of BR Mk1 and Southern Bulleid corridor stock c.1958. These venerable radial tanks were the mainstay of the branch's services for many years, No.448 is preserved on the Bluebell Railway in East Sussex. *Author's Collection*

South East England

The Lee-on-Solent Light Railway opened to traffic in 1894 and was part of a scheme to develop Lee-on-Solent as a new town by the sea. The railway was financed by a development company, who also had a similar scheme for a town on the Yorkshire coast, which did not get very far. The light railway was operated by the L&SWR on behalf of the owning company and ran from Fort Brockhurst to Lee-on-Solent. The railway was reluctantly taken over by the Southern Railway in 1923 and closed to passenger traffic in 1931, closing to freight in 1935. Here we see one of the L&SWR Manning Wardle 0-6-0 saddle tanks, normally used on engineer's trains, at the head of a train consisting of two of the centre entrance bogie carriages and a full brake parcels van at Fort Brockhurst c.1900. *Author's Collection*

The Totton Hythe & Fawley Light Railway was opened to traffic on 20 July 1925 by the Southern Railway and served an area along the coast leading to Southampton Water. In the late 1930s, an oil refinery was constructed at Fawley by the Anglo Persian Oil Company, which became the main source of traffic on the line, together with a military port at Marchwood, constructed in the 1940s. The line closed to passenger traffic in 1964 and to oil traffic in 2016 but is still open as far as Marchwood for military traffic. The picture depicts the opening day with an ex-L&SWR 02 class 0-4-4 tank, with one of the first trains entering Fawley station from Southampton. Author's Collection

The L&SWR opened the Basingstoke & Alton Light Railway in 1901, as a blocking line to prevent the Great Western Railway from penetrating into its area from Basingstoke towards the coast. During the First World War, the line was lifted as part of the war effort in 1917, but public pressure made the Southern Railway restore the line in 1924. However, the railway made little profit and was finally closed to passengers in 1932 and to goods traffic in 1937. It was immortalised in two pre-war films, when the line was used in *The Wrecker* and *Oh, Mr Porter!* Here we see a posed picture taken on the lines opening day with 02 class 0-4-4 tank No.203 and a train of four wheeled carriages on 1 June 1901, at Cliddesden Station. *Author's Collection*

Herriard station on the Basingstoke and Alton Light Railway c.1910, showing the corrugated iron building and run round loop. The infrastructure on this light railway was very basic, with minimal signalling, passenger and good facilities. *Author's Collection*

The Hundred of Manhood and Selsey Tramway was opened in 1897, constructed on private land without a parliamentary order. Promoted by Holman Fred Stephens, the line connected Chichester in West Sussex with Selsey on the coast, providing both local and seasonal transport for holiday visitors. The tramway became more official in 1924, when it changed its legal status and became the West Sussex Railway, closing to all traffic in 1935. Here we see Manning Wardle 0-6-0 saddle tank *Sidlesham* at Chichester station with a passenger working of an ex-Midland Railway van and two former Lambourn Valley Light Railway carriages c.1925. *Author's Collection*

The Ford Model T rail car set at Chalder station c.1930, the line had two such sets, the other being a Shefflex rail car unit. The stations were basic corrugated iron structures, like those found on the other Colonel Stephens lines, note the milk churns awaiting delivery, which might have just arrived on the rail car. *Author's Collection*

Manning Wardle saddle tank *Ringing Rock* at Selsey Shed in July 1927. The line had two former contractors' tanks constructed by this builder, *Sidlesham* of 1861 and *Ringing Rock* of 1883. *Photomatic*

The Shefflex rail car set at Selsey shed shortly after delivery in 1928, in its new fully lined livery; the four wheeled wagon at the rear was used for goods and milk churn traffic. These rail cars were not very comfortable to ride in, smelt of petrol and did a lot to drive passengers onto the local Southdown buses, rather than enhance the line's revenue. *Photomatic*

The Rye and Camber Tramway was opened in 1895, linking Rye with Golf Links and later Camber Sands, the line was constructed to 3ft gauge. This picture shows Bagnall 2-4-0 side tank locomotive *Camber*, constructed in 1895, coupled to the lines two bogie carriages, the Rother Iron Works example next to the locomotive and the rear vehicle being the Bagnall constructed carriage, here seen at Rye station c.1920.
A.W. Croughton

The Tram station at Golf Links, c.1900, showing the corrugated iron station building and run around loop, note the yard arm in the fenced area and the general bleakness of the area. *Author's Collection*

Camber Sands, with the Kent Construction Company Ex Simplex petrol tractor, acquired in 1925, with the Bagnall bogie carriage in the platform. The station was a timber constructed affair with a basic timber shelter, here seen in April 1931; the line closed in 1939 and was not reopened after the Second World War. *Photomatic*

The Rother Valley Railway, later the Kent & East Sussex Railway (K&ESR), was opened in April 1900, from Robertsbridge Junction to Tenterden later Rolvenden. It was extended to Tenterden Town in 1903 and further extended to Headcorn Junction in 1905. This is Rolvenden shed and works, where the locomotives and rolling stock were maintained c.1933, showing Hawthorne Leslie 2-4-0 tank *Northiam* constructed in 1899 and Ex-London, Brighton & South Coast Railway (LB&SCR) A1 Terrier No.3 *Bodiam*, inside the shed. *Author's Collection*

Ex-South Eastern & Chatham Railway (SE&CR) P Class 0-6-0 tank locomotive No.1556 at Tenterden Town Station, with a train made up of a single Ex-L&SWR bogie non corridor carriage, for Robertsbridge Junction c.1937. By the 1930s, the K&ESR was forced to hire locomotives from the Southern Railway, because its own fleet of aged motive power was not in a fit state for use on train services. 1556 was the first of many such hired locomotives, classes of which included P Class, A1X Terriers, O1 Class and 0395 Class. *Author's Collection*

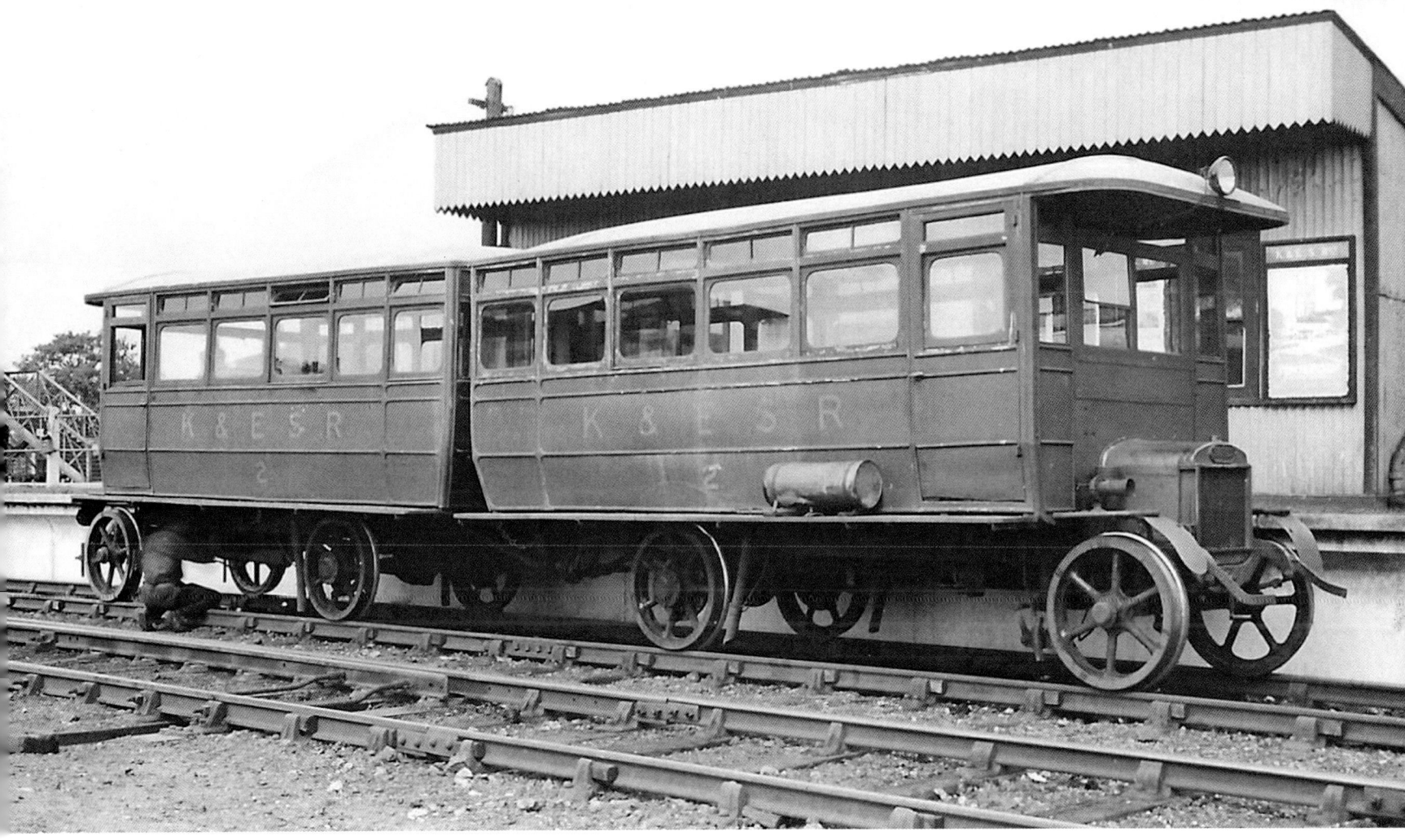

One of the ways the K&ESR tried to save money in the interwar period was to use petrol rail cars, here we see set No.2, constructed by Shefflex Motors of Sheffield in 1930, at Headcorn Junction station c.1933. They were not very popular with the passengers who quickly started to use local bus services. *Author's Collection*

A1X Terrier 0-6-0 tank No.3, formally named *Bodiam*, at Headcorn Junction on 8 May 1948, shortly after nationalisation, with a train of ex-L&SWR bogie carriage stock, bound for Tenterden Town. No.3 was rebuilt at St Leonards Depot near Hastings in 1943, using a spare A1X boiler from the Southern Railway. It became 32670 after nationalisation and is preserved today on the K&ESR. The K&ESR closed to passengers and to all traffic from Tenterden to Headcorn Junction on 2 January 1954 and to goods traffic on 12 June 1961. From Tenterden Town to Robertsbridge Junction, the former Rother Valley section is now a heritage line. *J.H. Aston*

Locomotives No.3, ex-L&SWR E0330 class 0394 of 1880 and Kerr Stuart Victory Class No.4 of 1917 at Shepherdswell locomotive shed, c.1938. Note the poor condition of the locomotive shed which was quickly closed after nationalisation in 1948. The East Kent Railway was opened in stages from 1912 to 1916 to serve the East Kent coal field, but as a result of geological problems and lack of finance, only one colliery opened at Tilmanstone near Shepherdswell. The line ran from Shepherdswell to Wingham Canterbury Road, with a branch to Richborough Harbour opened in 1925, passenger trains only running to Sandwich Road, both the main line and the Richborough line closed after nationalisation in 1948, passenger trains finishing in October 1948, to Wingham Canterbury Road and the Richborough line closing to goods services the same year. The goods service on the main line to Canterbury Road closed in stages in the early 1950s, with the final section from Shepherdswell to Tilmanstone colliery closing in the mid-1980s after the coal strike. *Ivor Gotheridge Collection*

Ex-L&SWR 0-6-0 saddle tank No.3, receives attention from the driver at Wingham Canterbury Road station c.1930, with a train of four and six wheeler carriages. This picture in so many ways sums up the atmosphere and general ambience of the British rural light railway, with its bucolic feel of a basic unkempt lonely station, miles from its village or town and a gypsy train of superannuated rolling stock. *Author's Collection*

A later view of Wingham Canterbury Road Station c.1938, showing the station building and the extent of the railway, which was meant to go on from here to Canterbury city, but never progressed any further, ending in a half finished cutting, beyond the sleeper on the track in the far distance. The East Kent Railway Closed in stages from 1948 to 1986 when the final section was closed due to the demise of Tilmanstone Colliery; the remaining section of the line is now a heritage railway. *Ivor Gotheridge Collection*

Eastchurch station on the Sheppey Light Railway, which opened in August 1901 and was engineered by Lt Colonel Holman Fred Stephens. This line served a largely rural community, being operated from its opening by the SE&CR and later the Southern Railway. It was only busy during both world wars, serving local military facilities, its local traffic being very light; it was finally closed in December 1950 by British Railways. *Author's Collection*

The Millwall Extension Railway was opened in 1871 for goods and 1872 for passenger traffic, linking North Greenwich and Millwall Dock Station. Originally horse worked, the line had converted to steam traction by 1880 and acquired six Manning Wardle 2-4-0 tank locomotives, which together with some Ex-GER four wheeled carriages were used to operate the passenger trains. The line operated a rapid turnaround service with regular trains every few minutes, however after the First World War, custom declined, despite the use of Ex-Great Western steam rail motors latterly, bringing about its closure after the General Strike in 1926. *Author's Collection*

The Lambourn Valley Light Railway was opened in April 1898 and was originally a wholly independent line, serving Newbury on the Great Western with Lambourn. The railway officially became a light railway in 1903 and was taken over by the Great Western in 1905, the line's main traffic being local produce and the transport of race horses, which were trained locally. The company had three locomotives, two constructed by Chapman & Furneaux in 1898 named *Eahlswith* and *Aelfred*, a third locomotive supplied by Hunslet followed in 1903 named *Eadweade*. The three locomotives were sold by the Great Western to the Cambrian Railways becoming their 26, 35, 24, before returning to the Great Western at the grouping in 1923. The line had a fleet of balcony end four wheel carriages, which were all purchased except one, by the Hundred of Manhood & Selsey Tramway. The line lasted through Great Western days and into the British Railways Western Region period, closing to passengers in January 1960 and goods in November 1973. 0-6-0 tank locomotive *Eahlswith*, departs Newbury with a train balcony end carriage stock for Lambourn c.1903. *Author's Collection*

The Wantage Tramway was opened in October 1875 and connected Wantage Road Station with Wantage Town in Berkshire. It operated a passenger and goods service, from its opening until closure to passengers in August 1925, closing to goods traffic in December 1946. The line made a profit throughout its existence and had close operating and financial links to the Great Western, who never tried to take it over. Wantage Tramway No.5 is seen here at Wantage Town c.1920, with the bogie tram car; staff and passengers pose for the camera. *Local Postcard*

The tram station at Wantage town, showing the platform and shelter for passenger services; one can see a former four wheeled horse tram in the distance, waiting for its next run to Wantage Road station August 1924. *Author's Collection*

After the Wantage Tramway closed to passenger traffic in August 1925, the tram engines and tram cars stood derelict in the sidings for some years before being broken up for scrap. Tram engine No.6, constructed by Matthews in 1882, coupled to tram trailer No.5 and the bogie tram car, May 1930. *Photomatic*

The Oxford and Aylesbury Tram road and Wotton Tramway was opened in April 1871, connecting Quainton Road Station with Brill in Oxfordshire. The line was constructed initially to serve the estate of the Duke of Buckingham, but soon developed into a passenger operation, which in 1899 was taken over and leased by the Metropolitan Railway who ran the main line to Verney Junction. The line became part of London Passenger Transport Board in July 1933 and was closed to all traffic in November 1935. The scene at Brill in 1935 with Metropolitan A class 4-4-0 tank No.23 and a single rigid eight wheeler brake carriage, about to depart for Quainton Road station. The station building is a basic timber structure, along with the timber platform, the locomotive shed can be seen behind the station. *Author's Collection*

Metropolitan A Class tank number 41 runs around its train in August 1932. This picture shows the locomotive shed and the other buildings at Brill to good effect, the derelict building between the small timber shed and the locomotive shed is the old forge, which had been out of use for some years at this time. *F.M. Gates*

Westcott Station in c.1934, showing the building and platform, with its oil lamps and rustic look. Colonel Stephens served part of his engineering training on the Metropolitan Railway and it is believed that he formulated many of his ideas for light railways from trips on the Brill Tramway. *Photomatic*

Wolverton & Stony Stratford Tramway was opened in 1886 by the London & North Western Railway to transport workers from Stony Stratford to the carriage works at Wolverton; it carried both passenger and goods traffic and became part of the LMS in 1923. The line was 3ft 6in gauge and operated double deck bogie tram cars. The tramway had made a loss for many years and was closed in 1926 to all traffic, at the time of the General Strike. Bagnall tram locomotive constructed in 1922 stands in the street at Wolverton, with a service to Stony Stratford in c.1924, note the size of the bogie tram car, which were the largest steam tram trailers in Britain. One is preserved in the Milton Keynes Museum. *Author's Collection*

East Anglia

Opened in 1901, the Corringham Light Railway ran from Kynochtown to Corringham in Essex, serving an explosives factory. Kynochtown became Coryton in 1921. The railway was owned by Kynochs, who produced Kynite explosive, which was used in the manufacture of ordinance for the military. The railway was connected to the London Tilbury & Southend Railway (LT&SR), having exchange facilities for the transportation of the explosive to all parts of Britain. After the First World War, the explosives factory closed down and the railway was sold to the oil industry, who developed the facility into an oil refinery and distribution facility. Here we see one of the Avonside 0-6-0 saddle tanks propelling an LNER wagon, while coupled to a train made up of former Midland Railway bogie carriage and four wheeled Ex-LT&SR composite vehicle at Corringham station c.1930.
Ivor Gotheridge Collection

Corringham Light Railway Avonside 0-6-0 saddle tank and Ex-LT&SR four wheeled carriage make up an enthusiast special on 17 May 1947, here seen at Corringham station. *Ivor Gotheridge Collection*

One of the original toast rack open sided bogie carriages, showing the tram like arrangement of seats c.1905; note the two plank open wagon on the far right. *Ivor Gotheridge Collection*

The Colne Valley and Helstead Railway was one of the larger minor railways in East Anglia, being opened on 16 April 1860 from Chapel & Wakes Colne in Essex to Haverhill in Suffolk; an extension was opened to Castle Hedingham in July 1861. The line linked with the Great Eastern Railway at both ends and was largely a rural operation handling farm produce, becoming part of the LNER at Grouping in 1923. The line was closed to passengers in 1962 and to goods traffic in 1965. There are preservation societies at Chapel Wakes Colne and at Hedingham. Here we see Hawthorn Leslie 1894 constructed 2-4-2 tank No.4 *Hedingham* c.1920, on a goods service. This locomotive was withdrawn by the LNER in September 1923. *Hopwood Collection*

Hudswell Clark 0-6-2 tank No.5 constructed in 1908, as a goods locomotive, at Halstead station c.1922, with a mixed train of ballast wagons and goods vans. This locomotive was withdrawn by the LNER in 1928. *Hopwood Collection*

Haverhill Stn, Goods Shed, and Carriage Shed.

Haverhill goods shed and station c.1910, showing the track layout and the basic station buildings. The timber building in the background next to the station is a one road locomotive shed, used to store locomotives overnight. *Local Postcard*

A J67 0-6-0 tank locomotive stands in the station at Kelvedon Low Level, on 12 August 1950 with a mixed train of bogie tram carriages and goods vehicles bound for Tollesbury. The Kelvedon, Tiptree and Tollesbury Pier Light Railway was projected and constructed by the Great Eastern Railway, opened in October 1904. The line served the local rural community and the famous jam factory at Tiptree, which gave the line most of its traffic. The line became part of the LNER at Grouping in 1923 and survived into the post nationalisation era, closed to passengers in May 1951 and to goods traffic from Tudwick Road to Tollisbury Pier in October 1951; the final closure came in October 1962.
John H. Meredith

The station at Tolleshunt D'Arcy c.1925 showing the low platforms for tram carriage operation and the neat timber building, with the grounded carriage body on the platform. *Local Postcard*

The Elsenham and Thaxted Light Railway was opened in April 1913, by the GER, serving a farming community in Essex. The line was never a great success as the stations were quite a distance from the places it served. The line was grouped into the LNER in 1923 and survived into early British Railways days, closing to passengers in September 1952 and goods in June 1953. Here we see an official picture of Thaxted station taken in 1913, at the time the line opened, showing all the benefits of the new light railway, including its arch rival in the form of the Ford Model T; note the grounded carriage body on the station platform, used as a goods store. *Great Eastern Railway Official*

Cutlers Green Halt in the last months of the Thaxted line in the autumn of 1952, showing the run down halt and dilapidated carriage body, used as a goods shed. *Author's Collection*

A Great Eastern 0-4-0 Tram Locomotive and train of tram trailers await passengers at the terminus of the Wisbech & Upwell Tramway c.1900. The Wisbech & Upwell Tramway was opened in August 1883, operating a service between the two locations, its main traffic being farm produce, closing to passengers in January 1928. The line survived through LNER days and well into the British Railways era, not closing to goods traffic until May 1966, when Drewry Diesel shunters had replaced the steam tram locomotives. *Local Postcard*

0-4-0 tram locomotive No.7132 runs through Outwell village with a train of empty open wagons in June 1929, a classic scene of a rural road side tramway, rare in Britain but commonplace on the continent of Europe. *Photomatic*

The Mid Suffolk Light Railway was opened to traffic from Haughley to Laxfield in September 1904 for goods, extended to Cratfield for goods in 1906, opened to passengers in September 1908. The company also constructed a goods only branch to Debenham in 1903. The line was originally meant to join up with the Southwold Railway at Halesworth, but this extension never occurred and the line was not extended beyond Cratfield. The line became part of the LNER at Grouping in 1923 and survived into the early 1950s under British Railways, closing to all traffic in July 1952. One of the three Hudswell Clark 0-6-0 tank locomotives, on a train of former Metropolitan Railway four wheel stock, here seen posed for an official picture in c.1908, at the time of the line's opening to passenger traffic. *Local Postcard*

Hudswell Clark 0-6-0 tank locomotive No.2 at Laxfield with a cattle train c.1908; this is an official posed picture to promote the newly opened line. Cattle traffic was an important part of the goods traffic on the Mid Suffolk Light Railway, as one can see from this illustration, along with farm produce. *Local Postcard*

A quiet scene at Mendlesham station c.1951, a year before closure of the light railway, showing the corrugated iron station building and the oil lamps on the platform. One of the Mid Suffolk Light station buildings has been rescued and can be found at Mangapps Farm on the heritage railway. *Author's Collection*

The Southwold Railway was a 3ft gauge railway linking Halesworth with Southwold on the Suffolk coast. Opened in September 1879, it operated a passenger and goods service for the local community for fifty years until April 1929 when it was closed. The scene is Southwold station c.1900 with one of the Sharp Stuart 2-4-0 tanks with a mixed train in the platform awaiting the signal to depart for Halesworth. *Author's Collection*

Sharp Stuart 2-4-0 tank No.3 Blyth arrives at Halesworth station c.1912, with a mixed train of open wagons and vans, the passenger carriages bringing up the rear. The carriages had a Cleminson arrangement for running gear, being six wheel vehicles, note the match wagon next to the locomotive. *Author's Collection*

The Welsh Borders and Midlands

The Bishops Castle Railway was a light railway by default, in that it started life as a main line project to construct a line from Craven arms to Montgomery. Opened in February 1866, the railway had constructed the first stage of its main line as far as Lydham Heath, where a junction was constructed so trains could run around and run to Bishops Castle on a branch line. As a result of the Overend Gurneys Bank collapse in that year, the Bishops Castle Railway was made bankrupt and never recovered, remaining a backwater minor branch line for all its existence. The company was in receivership from 1866 until the line closed in April 1935, despite several attempts to sell the railway to the L&NWR and the Great Western during that period. Locomotive No.1 at the head of a mixed train in Bishops Castle station c.1933, this former Great Western Armstrong 0-4-2 tank constructed in 1869, was the formally GWR 567, purchased in 1905; note the ex-Great Western brake van and the BCR Iron Mink van in train and the sidings. *Author's Collection*

In the shadows and light, *Carlisle* rests in the locomotive shed, awaiting its next turn of duty c.1934. Purchased in 1895, this Kitson 1861 constructed 0-6-0 tender goods, was used on several important contractors' jobs, before being sold on to the Bishops Castle Railway.

Originally, *Carlisle* had a four wheeled tender, which was replaced with a Great Western Armstrong tender during an overhaul at Wolverhampton works. It was *Carlisle* that worked the demolition trains after the line's closure in 1935 and into 1936, being cut up in the yard at Craven Arms, along with No.1, after the work was done. *Author's Collection*

Locomotive No.1 waits in the platform at Craven Arms, with a train consisting of the ex-Hull & Barnsley Railway four wheeled carriage and the former L&SWR, first, second and third class six wheeled brake vehicle c.1925. The Bishops Castle Railway had running rights from the junction north of Craven Arms to Craven Arms station, which was a L&NWR Great Western Joint operation. *W. Pooter*

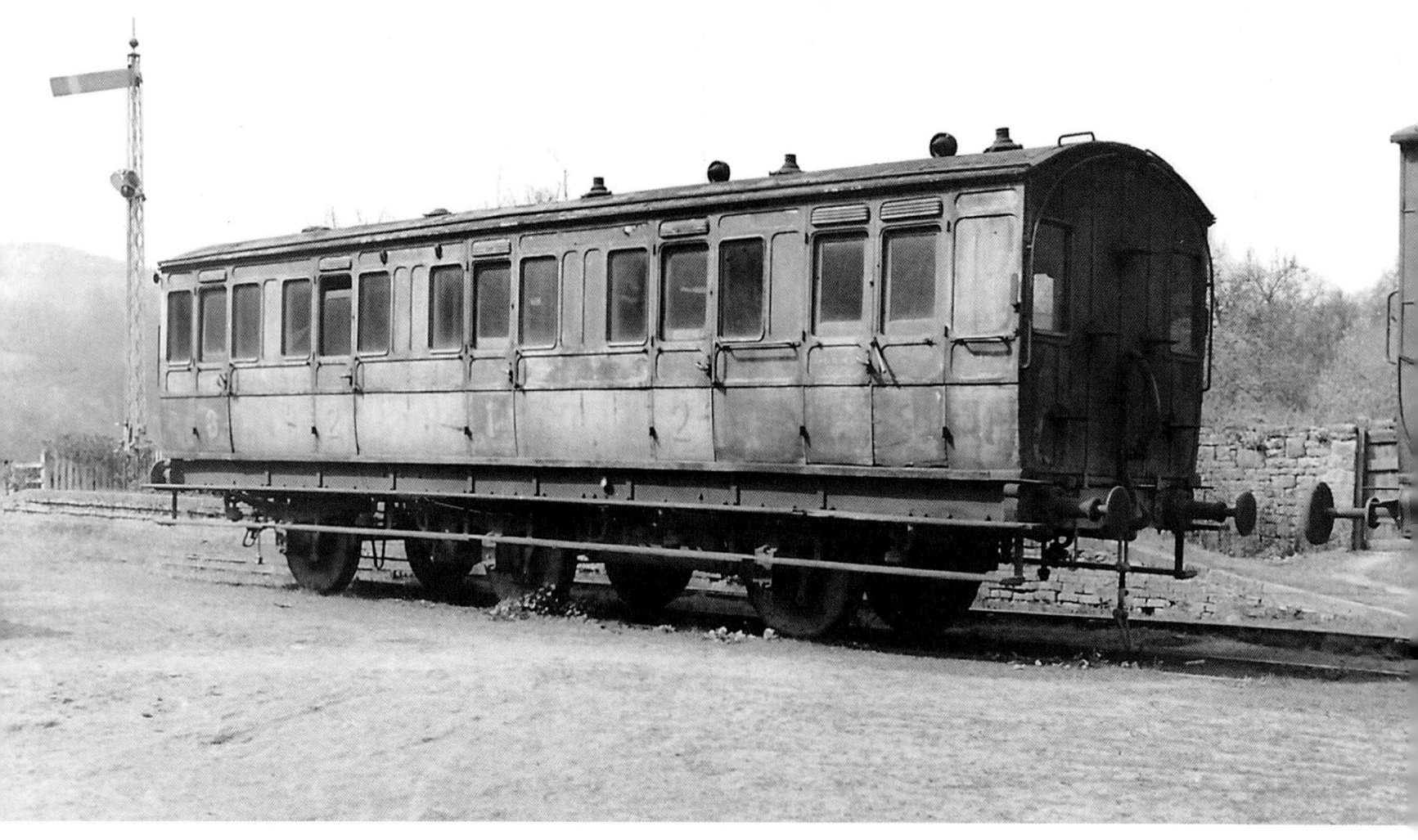

Ex-L&SWR six wheel first, second and third class brake carriage at Bishops Castle station, c.1934, looking very sorry for itself and in need of a coat of paint. Note the archaic signal in the background, installed in 1866 when the line opened; one of these signals can be found in the Bishops Castle Railway museum. *R.G. Jarvis*

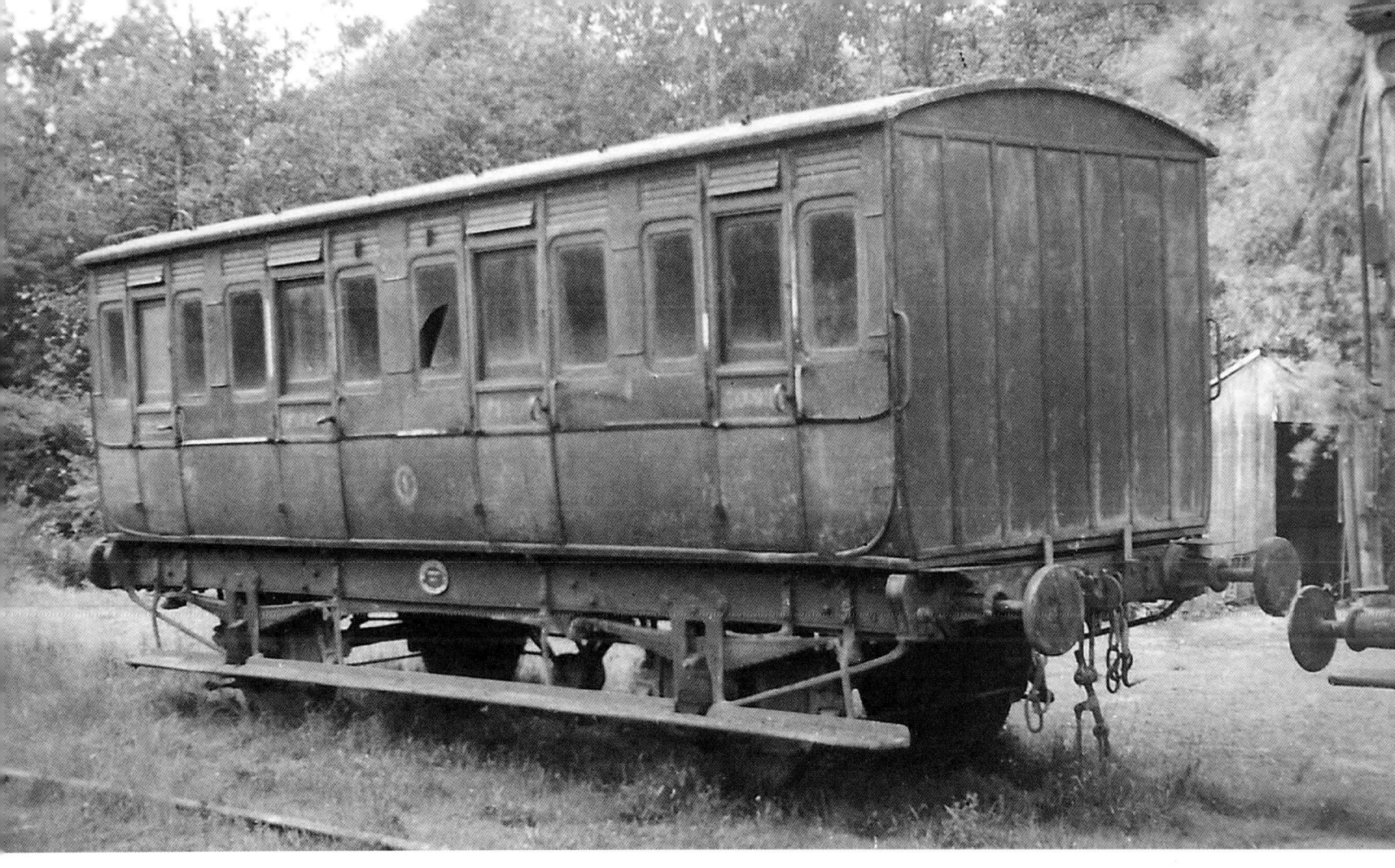

One of the three former L&NWR Clark and Webb chain brake carriages, which survived in traffic until 1924, here seen derelict at Plowden in 1935. The Bishops Castle Railway was the last railway in Britain to use this archaic form of braking, invented and used before vacuum brakes became commonplace. *Author's Collection*

The Snailbeach District Railway had an unusual gauge of 2ft 3¾in; opening in 1873, it served the lead mines around Stiperstones and Snailbeach in Shropshire. The line closed in 1915, but was reopened in 1922, when Colonel Stephens took over the railway and its operation. The line ran from Snailbeach to Pontesbury where it connected with a branch from Shrewsbury to Minsterley. Colonel Stephens inherited one locomotive, a Bagnall 0-6-0 tank named *Dennis*, which spent most of its life in store or dismantled as it was a very troublesome machine, with unusual valve gear which was hard to maintain, Here we see American Baldwin 4-6-0 No.3, constructed in 1915, purchased from the war disposals board in 1923, at Pontesbury exchange sidings c.1938, while shunting hopper wagons. *Author's Collection*

Locomotive No.2 was a Kerr Stuart Skylark Class 0-4-2 tank constructed in 1902, which we see hauling a long string of empty hopper wagons from Pontesbury to Snailbeach c.1935. This locomotive was used by the contractor while constructing the Leek & Manifold Light Railway in Staffordshire, before being sold to the Snailbeach District Railway. *Author's Collection*

The shed at Snailbeach with No.2 in steam with one of the two Baldwin 4-6-0 tanks Nos. 3 or 4; in the background one can see the second Baldwin 4-6-0 tank in the gloom of the shed in June 1943. All three locomotives wore out at the same time, which affected the operation of the railway, which by 1950s was leased to Shropshire County Council, who extracted road stone from the quarry, using a road tractor to haul the hopper wagons. *Author's Collection*

The scene at Snailbeach shed c.1928, with one of the Baldwin 4-6-0 tanks and the Kerr Stuart Skylark Class 0-4-2 tank outside the shed, the man standing next to the Baldwin locomotive is believed to be Colonel Stephens on an inspection visit to the line. The boiler barrel on the right hand side of the shed is from Bagnall 0-6-0 tank locomotive *Dennis* undergoing an endless overhaul, which was never completed.
F.A. Wycherley

One of the three ex-L&NWR 0-6-0 tender goods locomotives arrives at Kinnerley on the Shropshire & Montgomeryshire Light Railway, with a train of wagons for the quarry at Criggion c.1937. The Shropshire & Montgomeryshire Light Railway (S&MR) was opened in 1911 after reconstruction from the derelict Potteries Shrewsbury and North Wales Railway, which had been open from 1866 to 1880, closing as a result of bankruptcy and lying derelict for thirty-one years. The line ran from Shrewsbury Abbey station to Llanymynech, providing a through service across a sparsely populated rural area of the border between England and Wales. The Criggion branch reopened to the quarry from Kinnerley Junction in 1912, as a light railway with passenger and goods trains. *R.K. Blencowe Collection*

0-4-2 Well Tank locomotive *Gazelle*, on a rail tour in April 1939 at Llanymynech. This locomotive was constructed by Dodman of Kings Lynn in 1893, for a director of the Great Eastern Railway, who was allowed to run the locomotive on the main line, reaching York from Kings Lynn on one occasion. It was later sold to T.W. Wards of Sheffield, who sold it on to Colonel Stephens for use on the Criggion branch, along with an ex-LCC horse tram, which was purchased as a trailer, later replaced with the body of the Wolseley Siddeley rail car, reconstructed onto the tram chassis, as seen here. *Gazelle* was taken over by the Army in 1940 and used as an inspection locomotive and was later transferred to Longmoor camp in Hampshire for preservation. It is now on display at the Colonel Stephens Railway Museum in Tenterden, Kent. *F. Edmonds*

During the Second World War, the S&MR was taken over by the Army who constructed storage and munitions depots along the line, here we see a former Great Western Dean 0-6-0 Tender goods WD No.190 at Kinnerley shed in June 1947 between duties at the coaling stage. The Dean Goods locomotives were later replaced with Austerity saddle tanks, seeing operations on the line through to closure in 1960, when the army departed and Western Region closed the line. *Photomatic*

The Cleobury Mortimer & Ditton Priors Light Railway was opened in July 1908, linking the junction with the Great Western line from Bewdley to Tenbury Wells to Ditton Priors, serving a quarry there. The railway was later taken over by the Great Western at the Grouping in 1923, remaining open to passenger traffic until September 1938 and to goods traffic, in the form of munitions and stores for the Royal Navy, until 1966. Latterly, the line was operated by the RNAD, with its own diesel shunters from 1956 to 1966 as far as the junction at Cleobury Mortimer. The picture shows Manning Wardle 0-6-0 saddle tank *Cleobury* one of two identical locomotives, the other being *Burwarton*, on the line and brake van No.2, at Ditton Priors in 1908, shortly after the line's opening. *Author's Collection*

The station and stone quarry at Ditton Priors c.1910, showing the basic station building and track layout, with the quarry complex in the background. *Commercial Postcard*

The Great Western later reconstructed both the original Manning Wardle 0-6-0 saddle tanks, as pannier tanks at Swindon, No.28 formerly *Cleobury* stands with a mixed train including two Dean four wheel carriages at Cleobury Mortimer station c.1935, the other Manning Wardle *Burwarton*, became No.29, both lost their names after reconstruction. *Ivor Gotheridge Collection*

The Ashover Light Railway was a 60cm gauge line, opened in April 1925, using former War Department light railway equipment, locomotives and rolling stock. This distant view is of Ashover Butts station, showing its location and track arrangement c.1925, shortly after opening. The railway was owned by the Clay Cross Company, which owned quarries and was managed by Colonel Stephens on their behalf. The company had to provide a passenger service in order to obtain their light railway order, so four bogie carriages were ordered new from the Gloucester Carriage & Wagon Company for the opening. The passenger service ended in September 1936 and the line closed to stone traffic in March 1950. *Ivor Gotheridge Collection*

Baldwin 4-6-0 tank locomotive *Peggy*, at Clay Cross c.1930 with a passenger train for Ashover Butts. The locomotives were all American constructed Baldwin ex-War Department 4-6-0 tanks, named after the children of General Jackson, the chairman of the Clay Cross Company. In the background one can see the pipe works, which was served by the line and a complex of industrial sidings. *Author's Collection*

Peggy again, with a stone train of bogie ex-War Department open wagons near the quarry in c.1946. The railway and its rolling stock was getting very run down by this time as one can see from this picture; within four years the line closed and the company went over to road transport. *Ivor Gotheridge Collection*

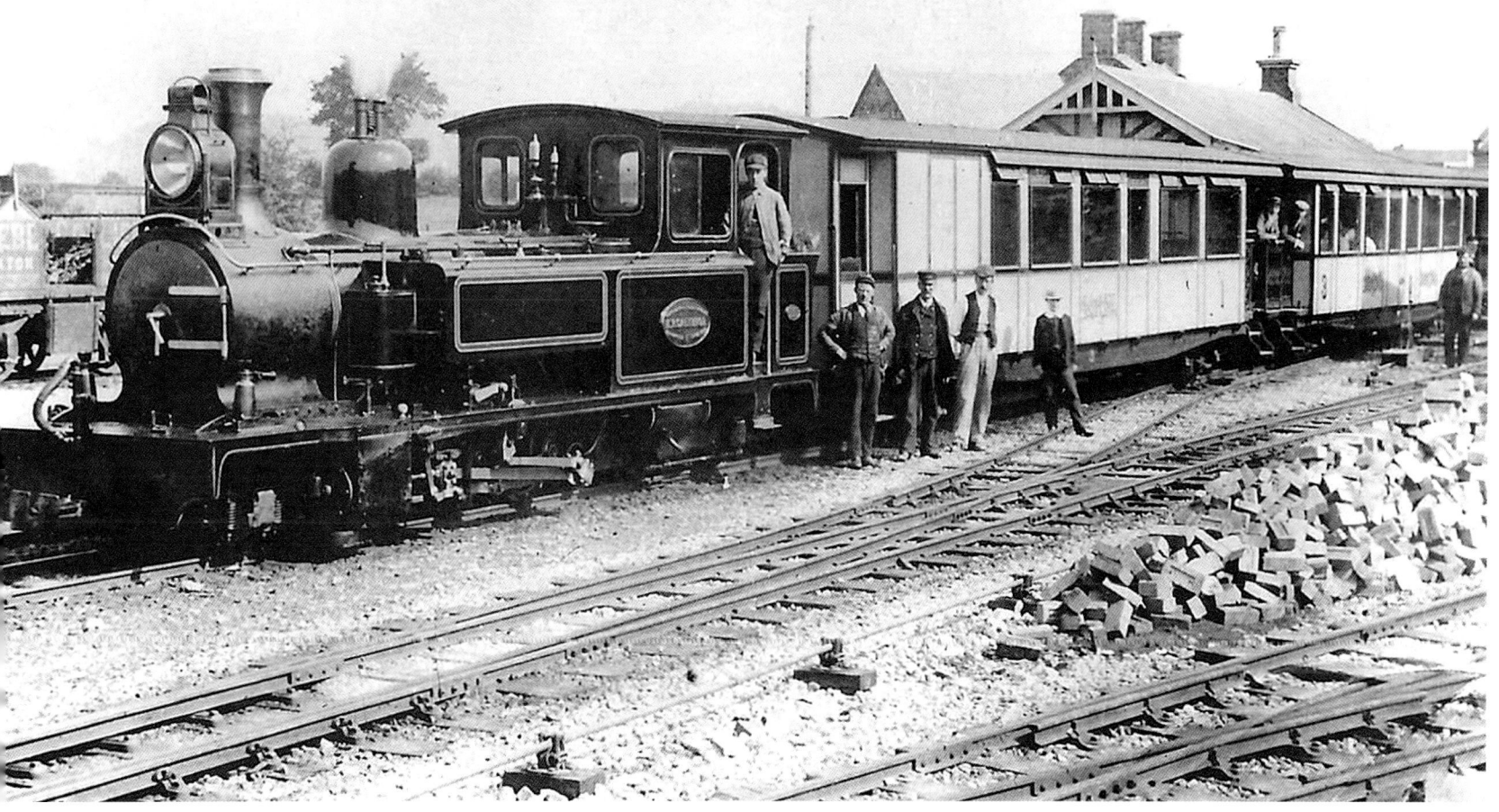

The Leek & Manifold Valley Light Railway served a scenic area of Staffordshire opening from Waterhouses on the North Staffordshire Railways branch from Leek and terminating at Hulme End in May 1904. The line's engineer was E.R. Calthrop who had constructed the Barsi Light Railway in India, which like the Leek and Manifold Light Railway had a gauge of 2ft 6in. The locomotives and rolling stock had a colonial look, almost a direct transplant from what you would expect to find in British India, the handsome Kitson constructed 2-6-4 tanks in lined madder red and the carriage stock in lined yellow livery. The railway served tourism and the local farming community, operating a passenger and local goods service, which did well when first opened, but declined after the First World War. The picture depicts a scene at Hulme End in 1904 just after opening, with a train of two new bogie carriages headed by Kitson 2-6-4 tank locomotive No.1, *E.R. Calthrop,* May 1904. *Commercial Postcard*

A second posed picture, taken at the time of opening in May 1904, showing 2-6-4 tank locomotive No.2 *J.B. Earle*, with a bogie brake third, there were four bogie carriages in the fleet of vehicles two brake carriages and two composites Bogie Brake First Third. *Commercial Postcard*

After the grouping in 1923 the line became part of the LMS, the picture depicts locomotive No.2, *J.B. Earle* at Hulme End station c.1930. The locomotives and rolling stock were painted in LMS livery by this time, the line closed and reopened in 1933, finally closing to all traffic in March 1934, the track being lifted in 1937 and the road bed being turned into a walking path. *Photomatic*

Ecton for Warslow station in May 1934, shortly after closure, showing the neat station building and ground level platform. *Photomatic*

An example of basic transport in the form of two of the bogie open wagons turned into open observation vehicles, c.1930. *Photomatic*

The Leek & Manifold Light Railway was noted for its converter wagons, which although common on the continent, especially in Germany and Austria, were only found on this line in Britain. Here we see a standard gauge eight plank coal wagon on one of the converter wagons being transported to its standard gauge siding, at one of the way side stations along the line.

A creamery along the line, was also served using converter wagons, to transport the milk tankers. *Author's Collection*

The North and North East of England

The Sand Hutton Light Railway was an 18in gauge privately owned line, constructed on private land owned by Sir Robert Walker. Opened in 1912 as a 15in gauge line to serve Sir Robert Walker's Estate, it was converted to 18in gauge in 1922, using four ex-War Department Hunslet 0-4-0 Well Tanks and rolling stock, also having a single bogie carriage, which was supplied new for the reopening. The railway ran from the LNER station at Warthill to Barnby House on the estate, with branches to a brick works at Claxton and a short branch to the hall, near Sand Hutton Central. The line opened to passengers and general goods, in October 1924 and was finally closed to all traffic in March 1932. Locomotive No.1 *Esme* is depicted with the new bogie carriage and brake van, in 1922, at the time of reopening. *Commercial Postcard*

A close up picture of the Sand Hutton bogie carriage and brake van c.1930, showing the balcony end and entrance arrangement. *Photomatic*

The Nidd Valley Light Railway was opened September 1907 to serve the project to construct a dam and water scheme at Angram, thirteen miles from the junction with the North Eastern Railway at Pateley Bridge. Although the line was a contractors' operation with small tank locomotives and wagons, there was for much of the line's existence a passenger service using second hand four wheeled carriage stock, for the workers on the water project and the local people. The railway was open for almost thirty years from 1907 until 1936, passenger services ceasing in December 1929. Here we see Avonside large saddle tank Blythe, constructed in 1922 at Pateley Bridge with a passenger service in the winter of 1928, a year before such services ceased, producing a plume of grey black smoke, that would make a modern day environmentalist very happy. *Photomatic*

The ex-Great Western steam rail motor, Hill, constructed by Kerr Stuart in 1905 and purchased by Bradford Corporation for use on the line in 1921, here seen at Lofthouse station c.1930. The steam rail motor was purchased for use on passenger services on the line, it was sold after the passenger services ceased in 1929, broken up in 1937. *Author's Collection*

Pateley Bridge locomotive shed in 1928, showing the Ex-Great Western steam rail motor and large Avonside saddle tank *Blythe* on shed. There were two locomotive sheds on the line, one a Pateley Bridge and a second shed at Ramsgill, which had an allocation of locomotives used on passenger trains. Both the shed building and the water tower are interesting timber structures and typify the line's contractor origins; the line is however properly signalled. *Photomatic*

Making heavy work of it, no less than four of the railway's locomotive fleet blast their way to the top of the incline near Wath in 1928. The first two locomotives being *Milner* constructed by Hudswell Clarke in 1909 for passenger services and Avonside constructed *Blythe* of 1922, the two saddle tanks at the rear are not recorded. Photomatic

The Garstang & Knott End Railway (G&KER) was opened in December 1870, as the Garstang & Catterall-Pilling Railway, however as a result of financial problems the line closed to all traffic in April 1872, only to reopen to goods traffic in February 1875, passenger traffic in April of that year. The line was extended to Knott End finally and opened in July 1908, by the Knott End Railway, which absorbed the original G&KER. The line was always short of finance and was finally taken over at the grouping in 1923 by the LMS, who operated the passenger service until March 1930, after which the line remained open to goods traffic. After nationalisation in 1948, British Railways closed the Knott End to Pilling section in November 1950 to goods traffic and the remaining section from Pilling to Garstang in July 1963. Here we see the Junction with the L&NWR at Garstang c.1908 with work in progress for improvements to the line, note the shed building in the distance and the island platform with the station building. *Local Postcard*

Preesall station shortly after opening in 1908, with Manning Wardle 0-6-0 tank *Knott End*, constructed in 1908, in the station with two of the balcony bogie carriages, waiting to depart the station, as the staff pose for the photographer. *Local Postcard*

L&NWR Ramsbottom 0-6-0 saddle tank No.1325 on hire to the G&KER, stands in the platform at Knott End station c.1914. The G&KER was not a well off railway and often had to hire in extra motive power at times of need. The train which consists of a passenger brake van and one of the balcony bogie carriages, awaits departure for Garstang, while the train crew pose for the photographer. *Local Postcard*

Probably one of the most unusual and ungainly light railway locomotives of all time, Manning Wardle 2-6-0 tank *Blackpool*, here seen with its crew c.1922; constructed in 1909, this strange locomotive did not last long into LMS days, being totally nonstandard it was withdrawn in 1924. *Author's Collection*

The Whittingham Hospital Railway was opened in 1889 and connected Whittingham Hospital in Lancashire to the jointly operated Longbridge Branch of the L&NWR and L&YR, at Grimsargh. The line was free to travel on and was used by patients and members of their family for visits, it also provided transport for supplies to the hospital and coal. After the Longbridge branch closed to passengers in 1930, the trains connected with the buses that served Grimsargh. The railway continued in use until June 1957, when it was decided to close the line and dispose of its assets, the track was lifted in 1958. Here we see Andrew Barclay 0-4-2 tank No.2, constructed new in 1904, at the head of a train of four wheeled carriages at Grimsargh station c.1935, awaiting departure for Whittingham. *Author's Collection*

Grimsargh Station showing the shelter and platform c.1950. There was a run around loop here, but not at Whittingham Hospital, trains having to be cable worked into a siding to facilitate a return journey. *Author's Collection*

Two of the locomotives used on the hospital railway; Andrew Barclay No.2, constructed in 1904 and ex-Southern Railway No.2357, Stroudley D1 0-4-2 tank constructed in 1886 formerly named *Riddlesdown* in LB&SCR days, here observed outside the locomotive shed at Whittingham in April 1951. The Stroudley D1 was named *James Fryers* on the Hospital railway, being withdrawn and replaced with a Sentinel four wheeled steam locomotive in 1956, after the D1 developed serious boiler defects. *Photomatic*

The Stroudley D1 0-4-2 tank stands in the station at Grimsargh c.1950, with a train made up of former LNWR brake vans, converted for passenger use with internal seating. *Author's Collection*

The Ravenglass and Eskdale Railway was opened as a 3ft 0in gauge line in May 1875, connecting Ravenglass on the Furness railways coast line from Whitehaven to Bootle, with the quarries at Beckfoot. The railway started a passenger service from November 1876, serving the local community and the growing tourist trade. The original company had mixed success and the line first closed in November 1908, to be reopened to stone and goods traffic in April 1911, only to close again in 1913. The line was re constructed to 15in gauge by Bassett Lowke in August 1915 and operated as a miniature tourist railway, from Ravenglass to Muncaster. From October 1915 it was extended to Irton Road and to Beckfoot in April 1916, the final extension being to Boot in April 1917. A new station was constructed at Dalegarth in 1922, where the line terminated, replacing the terminus at Boot, which was closed. The railway had two 3ft 0in gauge Manning Wardle 0-6-0 tanks, named *Devon* and *Nabb Gill* constructed in 1874; here we see *Devon* on a train of two four wheeled carriages passing the Stanley Ghyll Hotel c.1895. *Local Postcard*

Beckfoot station with its stone-built platform and basic timber shelter c.1900. *Local Postcard*

After the conversion of the line to 15 inch gauge in 1915, a number of Sir Arthur Heyward's locomotives from the Duffield Bank Railway were acquired by Bassett Lowke for use on the tourist line. They also worked at the quarry which was still open. Here 0-6-0 tank *Ella* hauls a train of stone to the crushing plant c.1924. *Photomatic*

Opened in June 1891, the Easingwold Light Railway was one of Britain's first light railways and it connected the North Eastern Railway at Alne with the town of Easingwold in Yorkshire. The railway operated a goods and passenger service for the locality and was not nationalised in 1948, having lost its passenger service in November 1948, finally closing to goods traffic in December 1957. Hudswell Clark 0-6-0 saddle tank No.2 constructed in 1903, simmers in the station at Alne with a mixed train for Easingwold only eight minutes away c.1938. *Author's Collection*

Easingwold station c.1935 with a train waiting to depart to Alne, headed by Hudswell Clark 0-6-0 saddle tank No.2 and a four wheel carriage. This picture shows the general station layout and track layout, also the old carriage body used as a goods store on the near left. *Author's Collection*

Locomotive No.2 at Alne c.1944 in wartime black livery. This was the second Hudswell Clark 0-6-0 saddle tank used on the line, the first being delivered for the opening in 1891 and named *Easingwold*; this was replaced by No.2 in 1903. The company hired a number of locomotives over the years including an 0-4-0 saddle tank when the line opened, not used on passenger trains, and later several 0-6-0 saddle tanks, when its own locomotive was away being overhauled. After No.2 was withdrawn in 1947, the company hired locomotives from the LNER and British Railways, mostly Ex-LNER, J72 0-6-0 tanks. *Photomatic*

A forlorn looking ex-North Eastern Railway six wheeled brake carriage stands in the station platform at Easingwold in the last year of the passenger service 1948. The Easingwold Railway started life with two ex-North Eastern Railway four wheel carriages in 1891, replacing them with two ex-North London four wheel vehicles and finally in 1936, with two former North Eastern carriages, of which this vehicle is one.
Author's Collection

The Derwent Valley Light Railway was opened in October 1912, linking York Layerthorpe with Cliff Common, on the North Eastern Selby to Market Weighton line. The light railway originally served the local farming community, but over the decades some important industries established themselves along the route of the line. The railway originally had a passenger service, which over the decades made a loss, especially after the First World War, when local buses started to make inroads to the line's profitability. Although the company operated local passenger services using locomotives hired from the NER and tried to cut costs with a Ford Rail car set, it was decided in September 1926 to close the line to passenger traffic. The line was operated as a freight only operation until it was gradually cut back, firstly from Cliff Common to Wheldrake in February 1965 and then Wheldrake to Elvington in May 1968, the final part of the line closing in September 1981. Here we see the Ford rail car set at York Layerthorpe station c.1924; this rail car set was sold in 1926 to the County Donegal Railway in Ireland and altered to 3ft gauge. *Photomatic*

The Derwent Valley Light Railway owned a Sentinel 0-4-0 locomotive for a period in the 1920s and early 1930s. It is seen in this picture shunting at York Layerthorpe station c.1930. *Photomatic*

Dunnington Station on the Derwent Valley Light Railway c.1928, showing the attractive arts and crafts style buildings and the platform, two years after closure to passengers. The Derwent Valley Light Railway remained independent throughout its entire existence, hiring locomotives from the NER, LNER and later British Railways to run its services. *Author's Collection*

The North Sunderland Light Railway was opened in August 1898 connecting Chathill on the NER line from Berwick to Alnmouth, with Seahouses on the North Sea coast. The light railway served the needs of the local coastal fishing community, providing a link with the main line and outside world and also served a quarry at Pasture Hill, reached by a short branch. The railway remained independent through the grouping in 1923 and even avoided being nationalised in 1948. The company had two of its own locomotives during its existence, these being a Manning Wardle 0-6-0 saddle tank named *Bamburgh* constructed in 1898 and later a pioneering 0-4-0 diesel locomotive named *Lady Armstrong*, constructed by Armstrong Whitworth in 1934. The company often hired locomotives from the LNER and in the final years from British Railways, North Eastern Region, normally in the form of Y7 class 0-4-0 tanks, also classes J79, J71, Sentinel Y1, Y3 and on one occasion an LMS Pug 0-4-0 saddle tank No.11217, which worked the line in 1948. Carriage stock came from the former Highland Railway in the form of five carriages in 1898, NER who provided two four wheeled carriages and on hire in LNER days a bogie motor fitted carriage, there were also in the final years three former Great Eastern Railway six wheel carriages. The picture shows a train at Chathill waiting to depart for Seahouses with a passenger train of former North Eastern carriages and a goods van c.1930. *Hopwood Collection*

The platform at North Sunderland, the only intermediate station on the line; this picture sums up the bleak nature of the area and the remoteness of this location. Note *Bamburgh*, the Manning Wardle 0-6-0 saddle tank in store on the siding middle right c.1948. *Photomatic*

Seahouses station in 1950, with a train headed by former LNER Y7, now British Railways No.68089, awaiting departure for Chathill with a train of two former GER six wheel carriages, note the locomotive shed in the distance. The railway closed to all traffic in October 1951.
Author's Collection

Lady Armstrong, the diesel shunter supplied to the line by Armstrong Whitworth in 1934. This locomotive was state of the art, cutting edge railway technology at the time, not what you would normally expect to find on a light railway, here seen at Chathill station with a train c.1935. *Author's Collection*

The South Shields Marsden & Whitburn Colliery Railway was a mixture of industrial and minor railway, opened in 1870 as a mineral line and diverted in August 1926 by a new coast road, when it officially became a light railway. The railway operated primarily as a colliery railway, which had a passenger service, used by the miners and the general public, which in 1947 became the first passenger railway to be nationalised in Britain. Locomotive No.7 was a Chapman & Furneaux 0-6-2 tank constructed in 1898. Originally used on passenger and mineral trains, it was later sold to the Pontop & Jarrow Railway. *Tom Middlemass Collection*

The second No.7 was Ex-LNER J21 0-6-0 Tender goods No.1616 purchased in 1930, here depicted at South Shields station, about to couple up to a passenger service to Whitburn, 9 June 1934. *Photomatic*

Locomotive No.5 was a former North Eastern Railway 398 Class 0-6-0 tender goods purchased in 1929, here seen hauling a heavy train of coal opens near Marsden Cottages c.1935. The company had a fleet of former NER 0-6-0 tender goods locomotives of different classes, purchased from the NER and the LNER over a long period of time. *Photomatic*

At South Shields, the network of lines servicing the collieries was electrified in 1908, this system linked the collieries at Westoe, St Hilda's, Harton and Bolden, with the coal staithes on the Tyne. The first electric locomotives and equipment were manufactured by Siemens, as some of the shareholders at this time were German and probably arranged a deal for the supply of the German electrical material. The scene depicts three of the original electric locomotives the two outer examples being four wheel and the centre locomotive being an eight wheel bogie locomotive c.1909. *Tom Middlemass Collection*

One of the four wheeled electric locomotives No.1, on 29 April 1952 at work at South Shields, electric locomotives have a long life span and this example had probably been working hard in the yards and sidings of the colliery complex for almost forty-five years, when this picture was taken. *Photomatic*

Wales

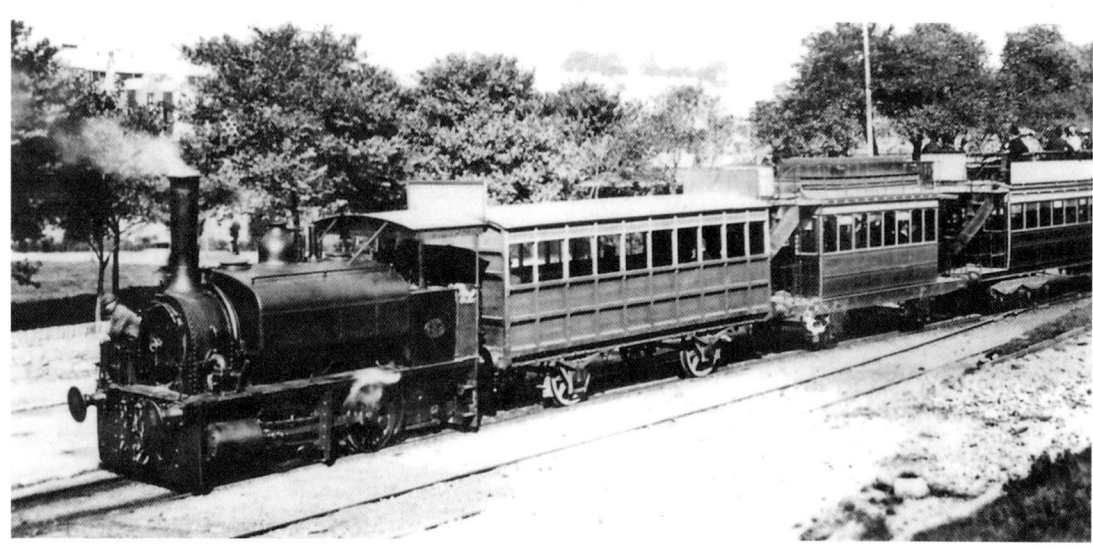

The Swansea & Mumbles Railway opened originally as the Oystermouth Railway in 1806, as a plateway conveying ore and running a passenger service using horse power, it was later upgraded to steam traction in 1877, when also the line from Blackpill to Oystermouth was abandoned and a new extension was opened to Mumbles Pier. The original horse operated passenger service ceased in 1826, when the line was relaid as a railway, not being reinstated as a passenger line until 1860. The railway had an intense steam operated service along its formation from Swansea to Mumbles Pier using small 0-4-0 and 0-6-0 tank locomotives hauling a string of four wheeled tram cars. The railway was electrified using bogie cars in 1929, the company became part of South Wales Transport bus operation and was closed in two stages, firstly the Mumbles Pier extension in October 1959 and the remainder of the line in January 1963. A Hawthorn Leslie 0-4-0 saddle tank No.2 heads a train of tram cars along the line c.1900. *Local Postcard*

The Burry Port & Gwendraeth Valley Light Railway started life as a mineral tramway linking Burry Port with Pembrey, embodying the earlier Kidwelly, Llanelli & Pembrey Harbour Tramroad. The line joined the Llanelli & Mynydd Mawr Railway at Sandy Gate, allowing for through mineral traffic. The railway was upgraded in 1909 and reopened as a light railway, Colonel Stephens being its engineer and consultant. The line was taken over by the Great Western in the 1923 grouping and passed to British Railways Western Region in 1948, closing to passengers in September 1953 and goods traffic in March 1998. 2021 class pannier 2067 stands at Burry Port station with a passenger service including two special low roofed bogie carriages and two Dean four wheelers on 7 August 1947. *Photomatic*

The Glyn Valley Tramway was opened April 1873 and operated a line from Chirk to Glyn Ceiriog, where the line went on to serve local slate quarries. The 2ft 4½in gauge steam tramway ran as a partial road side affair using Beyer Peacock constructed tram locomotives and four wheeled tram type carriages. The line provided local transport for many years along the Ceiriog valley, until its closure in July 1935. Tram locomotive *Sir Theodore* waits in the platform at Glyn Ceiriog station with a service to Chirk on 14 August 1925. *Author's Collection*

The 0-4-2 tram locomotive *Sir Theodore* again, with a service consisting of closed and open carriages at one of the wayside stations c.1910. This picture shows the features of the tram locomotive and rolling stock to good effect, including the all enclosed motion of the locomotive, surrounded in a steel skirt. *Author's Collection*

Tram locomotive *Dennis* runs on a raised section of the road side tramway, with a mixed train of passenger carriages and open wagons c.1925. *Photomatic*

The Baldwin 4-6-0 tank locomotive, obtained from the war disposals board in 1921; this 1917 constructed machine was obtained to strengthen the motive power in the post-First World War period and was useful on goods and slate trains. *Author's Collection*

The Welshpool & Llanfair Light Railway was opened in April 1903 connecting the town of Welshpool with the rural village of Llanfair Caereinon, serving the rural farming community. The line had two Beyer Peacock constructed 0-6-0 tanks and a set of three balcony end bogie carriages, supplied by R.Y. Pickering, along with a selection of four wheeled goods wagons. The light railway was originally operated for the company by the Cambrian Railways, but was absorbed into the Great Western at grouping in 1923, closed to passenger traffic in February 1931, becoming part of the Western Region of British Railways at Nationalisation in 1948. After the line closed to all traffic in November 1956, a preservation society was formed and saved most of the line except the section from Welshpool to Raven Square, where the heritage line now has its terminus. The picture depicts locomotive No.1 *The Earl* posed with a train of timber flats at Welshpool goods yard shortly after opening in 1903. *Author's Collection*

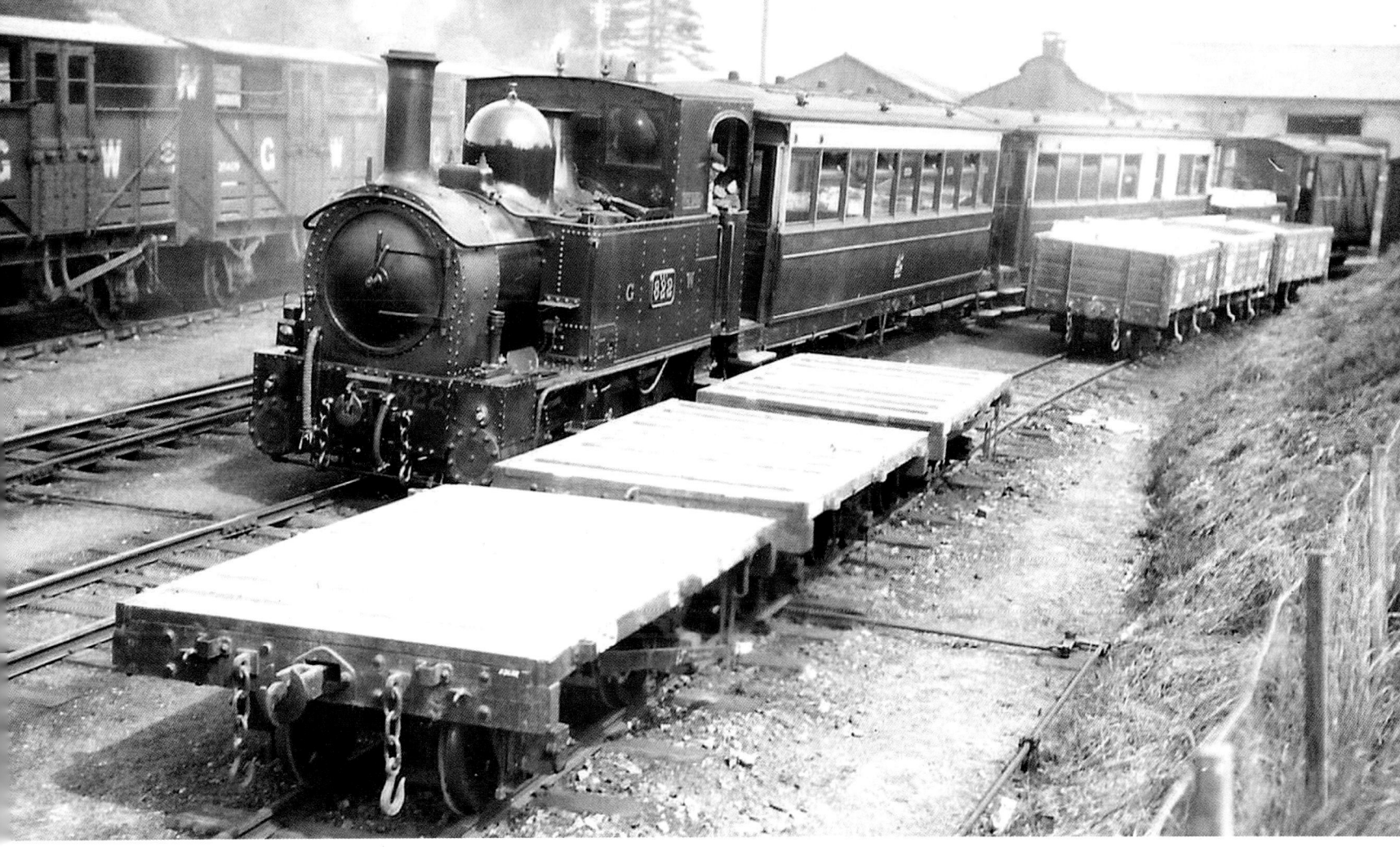

The Earl again as Great Western 822 passing Welshpool Yard with a mixed train service c.1930 after rebuilding at Swindon works with a new boiler and fittings. This picture shows the main line goods yard with a line of cattle wagons and the 2ft 6in Welshpool & Llanfair yard with a selection of open and flat wagons. *Author's Collection*

The Mawddwy Railway, promoted by Sir Edmond Buckley, who wished to develop the village into a prosperous town, opened in October 1867, serving a rural community at Dinas Mawddwy, the standard gauge line also served local slate quarries in the Aberangell district. The line ran from Dinas Mawddwy to Cemmaes Road on the Cambrian Railways main line to Aberystwyth from Shrewsbury. The railway originally had two Manning Wardle contractors 0-6-0 tank locomotives named *Mawddwy* and a larger machine named *Disraeli*, which along with some second hand carriages operated the passenger services. The railway closed to passengers in April 1901, and to goods in April 1908, but was reopened by the Cambrian Railways as a light railway in July 1911. The line was taken over by the Great Western at Grouping in 1923, closed to passenger services in January 1931 and under British Railways Western Region to goods in July 1951. The scene at Dinas Mawddwy station c.1912, with a Cambrian Railways goods van standing in the platform. *Author's Collection*

The 2ft 3in gauge Corris Railway started life as the Corris Machynlleth & River Dovey Tram Road in April 1859, operating a horse tramway from the slate quarries in the Aberllefenni, Upper Corris and Llwyngwern areas of the Dulas Valley to a quay at Derwenlas on the river Dovey, where slates were shipped in schooners across the world. The railway was taken over in 1878 by Imperial Tramways based in Bristol, who modernised the line and relaid it with heavier track, also introducing three Hughes 0-4-0 saddle tank locomotives and a passenger service with four wheeled tram carriages. The company later replaced the tram carriages with eight bogie carriages in the 1890s to cater for the growing tourist trade, operating horse wagonette and later petrol bus services in the area. The railway was taken over in 1930 by the Great Western who withdrew the passenger services in January 1931. The Corris Railway survived the war as a slate and goods line, to be closed to all traffic in August 1948, by British Railways Western Region. Kerr Stuart 0-4-2 Saddle Tank Number 4, Constructed in 1921, runs over the second river Dovey Bridge c.1938 with a goods and slab wagon train bound for Aberllefenni. *Author's Collection*

The Friday afternoon slate quarrymen's passenger service is about to arrive at Llwyngwern station, with a Hughes 0-4-2 saddle tank heading a train of bogie carriages, bound for Machynlleth; the quarrymen in this picture would use this train to return home for the week end, returning on Sunday evening to resume their arduous work in the quarries on Monday c.1897. *Author's Collection*

Maespoeth Junction looking towards Corris c.1925, showing the locomotive shed and lean-to carriage shed, with one of the bogie saloons undergoing repairs. This was the shed and works for the lines motive power, which by then was down to two steam locomotives, No.3 a Hughes Falcon 0-4-2 saddle tank of 1878 and a Kerr Stuart 0-4-2 saddle tank of 1921; both still exist on the Talyllyn Railway. *Author's Collection*

Corris station with its overall roof, which housed on the right a carriage shed and on the left the station and through platform, looking towards Aberllefenni in April 1946. The Corris Railway Society now runs a passenger service using replica rolling stock and locomotives from here south to Maespoeth Junction, which operates during the year from spring to autumn. *R.E. Tustin*

Horse shunting at Aberllefenni Quarry c.1946, with slab wagons being hauled forward from the slate quarry cutting shed to the Corris main line at Aberllefenni station, echoes of the early days when such operations were carried out as far as Derwenlas Quay. *Author's Collection*

The 1ft 11½in gauge Vale of Rheidol Light Railway was opened in December 1902, connecting the coastal town of Aberystwyth with Devil's Bridge, a popular tourist spot. The line served the needs of tourists and the lead mining industry in the Rheidol Valley, which was still in full production in the early twentieth century. The independent railway was taken over by the Cambrian Railways in July 1913 and continued under their control until the railway grouping in 1923, when the line became part of the Great Western. The lead mining industry had ceased by this time and the railway operated a passenger service throughout the year, until January 1930 when a summer's only service was commenced. Goods traffic was also curtailed during the 1930s, the harbour branch being closed in 1933 and traffic centered on tourist services, until 1940 when the line was closed for the duration of the Second World War. The railway opened up again in 1945 and continued through the British Railways period, firstly managed by Western Region and from 1963 by the London Midland Region. In each case an attempt was made to close the line, however due to public pressure this did not take place. The railway was privatised in 1989 and is now owned by a trust, which operates the line as a tourist and heritage railway. Here we see locomotive No.3 *Rheidol*, constructed by Bagnall in 1896, originally for a plantation railway in Brazil. As the original order failed it was sold to the Plynlimon and Hafan Railway, where it was named *Talybont* and then *Rheidol*. During a period of six years the locomotive had its gauge altered three times. We see No.3 at the original Aberystwyth station in c.1905 with a short train of a single bogie carriage and a four wheeled brake van. *Author's Collection*

Aberystwyth station in the mid-1930s with one of the two recently constructed Great Western 2-6-2 tanks No.1213 constructed in 1923 at the head of a tourist train to Devil's Bridge. The other 2-6-2 tank was 1212 also constructed at Swindon in 1923, to replace the two original prairie tanks designed by Davies & Metcalf in 1901. One of the original 2-6-2 tanks No.2 was reconstructed at Swindon in 1923, all three became No.7 *Owen Glyndwr*, No.8 *Llewelyn* and No.9 *Prince of Wales* in 1956 under British Railways. *Author's collection*

A mixed train of passenger bogie carriage stock and open wagons runs down the valley from Devil's Bridge in this mid 1920s picture, during the time when goods was still handled by the line. *Photomatic*

One of the Davies & Metcalf prairie tanks and Bagnall 2-4-0 tank No.3 wait at Devil's Bridge terminus, on a blustery day c.1910, with trains for Aberystwyth. *Local Postcard*

The Talyllyn Railway was constructed to 2ft 3in gauge and opened in 1865, serving the slate quarry at Bryneglwys and serving the village of Abergynolwyn, with a line from the coastal town of Towyn. The railway introduced passenger trains in 1866, with three four wheeled carriages supplied by Brown Marshall and later a fourth vehicle supplied by Lancaster Carriage and Wagon Company. The locomotives were both supplied by Fletcher Jennings of Whitehaven, No.1 being an 0-4-2 saddle tank named *Talyllyn* and No.2 being an 0-4-0 well tank named *Dolgoch*, which during the Anglo Boer War was named briefly *Pretoria*. The line led a quiet existence and was forgotten in 1948, when nationalisation took place, being the first railway in the world to be preserved as a heritage line, run by volunteers. Today it is one of the great little trains of Wales and transports many thousands of tourists along its formation. Here we see the station at Towyn Wharf c.1912, with the station building and yard, with lines of slate and open wagons waiting to be worked back up the line to the quarry. *Author's Collection*

Locomotive No.1 *Talyllyn* arrives at Towyn Wharf c.1925, with a passenger train from Abergynolwyn. The young lad is sitting on the running board of the ticket office brake van, supplied in 1866 by Brown Marshall for the opening of the line. *Author's Collection*

Dolgoch No.2 stands on a wet day at Rhydyronon station with a train for Abergynolwyn; the train formation consists of all four carriages, c.1946. The railway was owned and constructed originally by the McConnel family from Manchester but was later sold to Sir Haydn Jones, a local MP and quarry owner, who also had interests in the Corris area. It was his family who agreed to allow the preservationists to save the line in 1951, after Sir Haydn Jones died. *Author's Collection*

One of the Brown Marshall four wheeled carriages at Abergynolwyn station c.1910; these carriages are still in use today and are used on the Talyllyn Railways vintage trains. *Hopwood Collection*

The Festiniog Railway was opened in 1836 as a horse drawn railway serving the quarries at Blaenau Festiniog and connecting the slate traffic to the sea at Port Madoc harbour. The horses hauled the slate wagons up the line from Port Madoc to the quarries and the loaded wagons were made up into trains and gravity worked back to the harbour, the horse riding in a dandy car. After the Spooner family became involved in the 1860s, things began to change and modernise. In 1863, steam traction was introduced with George England constructed 0-4-0 tender locomotives, *Princess* and *Prince*, which led to a fleet of 0-4-0 tender locomotives and later single and articulated double Fairlie 0-4-0 0-4-0 type locomotives, which hauled both passenger and goods trains. Here we see George England 0-4-0 tender locomotive No.4 *Palmerston* at Portmadoc Harbour station c.1925, heading a passenger train of four wheeled and bogie carriage stock. This locomotive is now preserved and occasionally used on the heritage line. By this time the line was managed by Colonel Stephens, who did not always get on with the locals, who did things their way. *Local Postcard*

Tanybwlch station c.1900 with a double Fairlie locomotive on a passenger train of bogie stock bound for Portmadoc, passing a mixed train of passenger stock and empty slate wagons, heading for the quarries at Blaenau Festiniog. Note the early slotted semaphore signal on the right and the station building on the upper right. *Local Postcard*

Locomotive No.4 *Palmerston* and the simplex tractor now named *Mary Ann*, at Boston Lodge works c.1930. The armoured Simplex tractor was acquired by Colonel Stephens together with an American Baldwin four wheeled petrol locomotive from the war disposals board in the early 1920s in order to make economies on the line. Both machines survived to be preserved by the preservation society and are still in use. *Author's Collection*

One of the early bogie carriages in its original ornate lined livery, here seen at Boston Lodge works c.1895. These carriages were introduced in the 1870s and some examples survive to day on the heritage line. The balcony ends are designed to allow passengers to traverse the carriage at stations and allow in this case the guard to board the train through the door in the centre of the balcony. *Author's Collection*

Slate wagons being unloaded at RHYD DDU c.1925. The Great Western owned a sizable fleet of these wagons which it constructed itself in its wagon workshops. *Author's Collection*

The North Wales Narrow Gauge Railway was opened to goods from Dinas Junction to Quellyn in May 1877, opening to passengers to Snowdon Ranger in August 1877 and Rhyddu in May 1881. A branch was constructed from Tryfan Junction to Bryngwyn opened August 1877 to serve local slate quarries. This line was not a total success and was closed to passenger traffic by December 1913. During the First World War the line closed down and did not reopen after the war in its original form, being reconstituted as the Welsh Highland Railway, reopening the line from Dinas Junction to South Snowdon in July 1922 to Beddgelert and Portmadoc in June 1923, using part of the Croesor Tramway to arrive at Portmadoc where it joined the Festiniog Railway. A single Fairlie 0-6-4 tank locomotive and train of bogie and Cleminson carriage stock stand at Snowdon Ranger station c.1885. *Local Postcard*

Beddgelert station looking towards Dinas Junction, c.1924, showing the basic corrugated iron station building and passing loop; this is probably the most spectacular part of the line through the Aberglaslyn Pass with its impressive views. *Local Postcard*

Beddgelert station again with Hunslet 2-6-2 tank *Russell* and Baldwin 4-6-0 tank 590 on trains bound for Dinas Junction c.1934. Note the carriage next to *Russell* which is the former North Wales Narrow Gauge Railway observation car. *Russell* was by this time cut down with a short chimney, dome and cab, in order to run trains from Dinas Junction to Blaenau Festiniog. It was not a success, as the locomotive could barely get through Moelwyn Tunnel, scraping the sides, which was only attempted once. *Local Postcard*

Russell again, at Dinas Junction station waiting with a train for Portmadoc in 1935; one can see from this picture the ugly rebuilding of this once elegant locomotive, a task badly executed for an ill-thought-out project. Happily, *Russell* is now restored to its beautiful former glory and is often used on heritage trains on both the Welsh Highland and Ffestiniog Railways. *Author's Collection*

The Snowdon Mountain Railway is Britain's only traditional rack and pinion railway. Connecting Llanberris with Snowdon Summit, it opened in April 1897; the line had a bad accident on the first day when a train derailed and toppled over, however the railway has since then enjoyed a successful existence ferrying many thousands of tourists to the summit of Snowdon each year. The line is a traditional Swiss style rack and pinion line, using Swiss constructed 0-4-2 tank locomotives manufactured by Swiss Locomotive Works at Winterthur and bogie carriage stock. Today there is in addition to the steam fleet a number of diesel locomotives in use on this iconic line. This picture shows locomotive No.4 *Snowdon* on a single carriage train of the original open sided stock c.1900, stopped at one of the wayside stations waiting for a descending train to pass, before continuing to the summit. *Local Postcard*

Locomotive No.5 *Moel Siabod* at one of the way side stations c.1925 waiting with a train, while some of the passengers enjoy the sunshine and admire the rack locomotive. *H. Gordon Tidey*

Scotland

The 2ft 3in gauge Campbeltown & Macrihanish Light railway was Scotland's only independent light railway, connecting Campbeltown with Macrihanish on the Argyll Peninsula. Opened in 1877 for coal traffic and 1906 for passenger services, it was later rebuilt and served as a passenger line with two impressive Andrew Barclay 0-6-2 tank locomotives, *Argyll* and *Atlantic*, constructed in 1906 and 1907 respectively, a Kerr Stuart Skylark class 0-4-2 tank named *Princess* and two Andrew Barclay 0-4-2 tanks, one a well tank named *Pioneer* constructed in 1875 and a second 0-4-2 saddle tank locomotive named *Chevalier*, which was the original locomotive owned by the Campbeltown Coal Company, constructed in 1885. Apart from local passenger and goods traffic, its only other revenue came from the local colliery, owned by the Duke of Argyll. The railway had a fleet of handsome bogie carriages with balcony ends and a large number of open wagons for coal and local traffic. The railway was successful until the late 1920s, when bus competition and the closure of the colliery spelt the end for the line, which closed to all traffic in September 1931. One of the Andrew Barclay 0-6-2 tanks waits with a passenger service to Macrihanish in the street terminus at Campbeltown c.1928. *Tom Middlemass Collection*

Andrew Barclay 0-6-2 tank Atlantic simmers at the terminus at Machrihanish c.1928, with a train of bogie carriage stock while waiting to return to Campbeltown. *Photomatic*

The Andrew Barclay 0-4-2 Saddle Tank *Chevalier* at the colliery c.1925; this machine was the second 0-4-2 tank locomotive on the line constructed in 1885, the first being *Pioneer* constructed in 1875. Note the dome cover from the Kerr Stuart 0-4-2 tank *Princess* in use as a sand box. *Tom Middlemass Collection*

Ireland

The Timoleague and Courtmacsherry Light Railway was opened in April 1891 connecting the two towns, The company was in fact two separate concerns originally, the Timoleague and Courtmacsherry Light Railway and the Ballnasearthy and Timoleague Junction Light Railway, which operated the line. The light railway was Ireland's last roadside tramway and served the local rural farming community. It was taken over by the Great Southern Railways in 1925 and became part of CIÉ in 1945, having its passenger service withdrawn in February 1947.
It then soldiered on until 1960 when its goods service ceased to operate without warning; the line was never reopened. Here we see Hunslet 2-6-0 tank *Argadeen* at Courtmacsherry station c.1920 with a passenger service to Timoleague.
Hopwood Collection

There were three locomotives on the Timoleague and Courtmacsherry Light Railway, *Slaney,* an 0-6-0 saddle tank, *St Molaga*, an 0-4-2 tank and *Argadeen,* a 2-6-0 tank, all Hunslet products. All three locomotives became part of the GSR locomotive fleet and *St Molaga* and *Argadeen* lasted into CIÉ days. Here we see *St Molaga* on the shed yard at Cork c.1950 shortly before its withdrawal. *Tom Middlemass Collection*

The Cork Blackrock & Passage Railway started life in 1850 as a 5ft 3in gauge line connecting the City of Cork with Passage, six miles from Cork. It was later, in narrow gauge days, extended to Crosshaven on the coast. It operated a local service for goods and passengers, which doubled as an early form of city commuter service for those who worked in Cork. The line originally had three 2-2-2 Well Tanks all constructed by Sharp Brothers in 1850, No.2 later being reconstructed as a saddle tank, and also had a fleet of four wheeled carriages, all scrapped in 1900. The line was converted to 3ft 0in gauge in 1900, completely re-equipping with a fleet of four smart looking 2-4-2 tank locomotives constructed by Neilson Reid and an equally modern fleet of bogie carriage stock. The line was something of an intense service railway operating a fast regular train service on a well-maintained double track railway. The railway became part of the Great Southern Railways in 1925 and was closed to all traffic in 1932. One of the 2-4-2 tank locomotives simmers at the head of a train of bogie stock at Cork station c.1930, note another 2-4-2 tank in store in the siding far right, behind the train of open wagons. *Tom Middlemass Collection*

Three of the Neilson Reid 2-4-2 tank locomotives after the Great Southern Railways take over, on 10 June 1932 shortly before the lines closure, No.6P heading the line-up, all four locomotives found a new home on the Cavan & Leitrim Railway in the North East of the Irish Free State. *Photomatic*

Falcon works, constructed in 1898, Cork & Muskerry 4-4-0 tank No.7 formerly named *Peake,* here seen being serviced at Cork c.1930. The 3ft 0in line opened August 1887 from Cork to Blarney and was extended with branches to Donoughmore in May 1893 and to Coachford in March 1888, being absorbed into the Great Southern Railways in 1925 and closed due to road competition in December 1934. *Tom Middlemass Collection*

An unidentified Falcon 4-4-0 tank leaves Cork terminus with a passenger service c.1928 consisting of bogie carriage stock. The line was slowly declining by this time owing to road competition, even though in former years it had served a thriving tourist industry. *Hopwood Collection*

The 3ft 0in Schull & Skibberine Railway was opened in November 1886. Running from Schull to Skibbereen via Kilcoe, the railway was a rural roadside tramway, operating passenger and goods services. The line was taken into the Great Southern group of railways in 1925 and survived long enough to become part of CIÉ in 1945, finally closing completely as a result of a coal shortage in 1946. One of the 4-4-0 tanks, No.4 named *Erin*, constructed by Nasmyth Wilson in Eccles Manchester in 1888, stands at the head of a mixed train of a bogie balcony end carriage and four wheeled vehicle, behind which are a mixed selection of goods vans and an open wagon c.1910. *Tom Middlemass Collection*

Erin again, this time outside Schull locomotive shed as GSR No.4S c.1935, by this time the locomotives were painted black and had been fitted with cast number plates. *Lens of Sutton Collection*

Hunslet constructed 4-6-0 tank Locomotive No.3C takes water at Ennis station on the 3ft 0in gauge West Clare Railway c.1950. The West Clare Railway was opened from Ennis to Milltown Malbay in July 1887, the line extended to Kilkee and Kilrush in 1892, August for goods traffic and December for passenger. As with all the other narrow gauge Irish lines, the West Clare became a part of the GSR in 1925 and again a branch of the CIÉ in 1945. Although the line was dieselised in the mid-1950s with rail cars for the passenger services and diesel locomotives for the goods services, it still made a considerable loss and it was decided by CIÉ to close the line completely, which took place in February 1961.
Tom Middlemass Collection

Ennis station on 4 February 1950 showing the general station track layout and a cattle train waiting in the platform, while over on the far right a train of WCR bogie carriages stand in the bay platform. *T.J. Edgington*

Moyasta Junction with the lines to Kilkee on the right and Kilrush on the left, the two home signals stand sentinel awaiting the next service to Ennis, while a Walker rail car waits in the platform of the line to Kilkee c.1959. *Author's Collection*

A Walker rail car waits in the platform in August 1957 at Kilrush. The introduction of these rail cars and the use of diesel locomotives on cattle and goods trains did not save the line which closed three years later. *Henry Townley*

The Listowel & Ballybunion Railway was Ireland's only monorail, opened in March 1888. The company who owned it was truly international, in that the Lartigue system used was French, the line's engineer was German and it was owned by a British company operating a railway in Ireland. The iconic railway has become part of Irish folklore and a museum exists in Ballybunion that celebrates the line, with a working replica petrol driven locomotive and carriages, giving short rides. The line suffered during the civil war in the early 1920s and was not taken into the GSR group, closing to all traffic in 1924. The scene is at Ballybunion, showing the station sheds and point system for the monorail. There were three locomotives on the line, one being an upright boilered shunting locomotive and the other two being constructed by Hunslet of Leeds; this is Hunslet 0-2-0 No.1, with its large headlight c.1888. *Hopwood Collection*

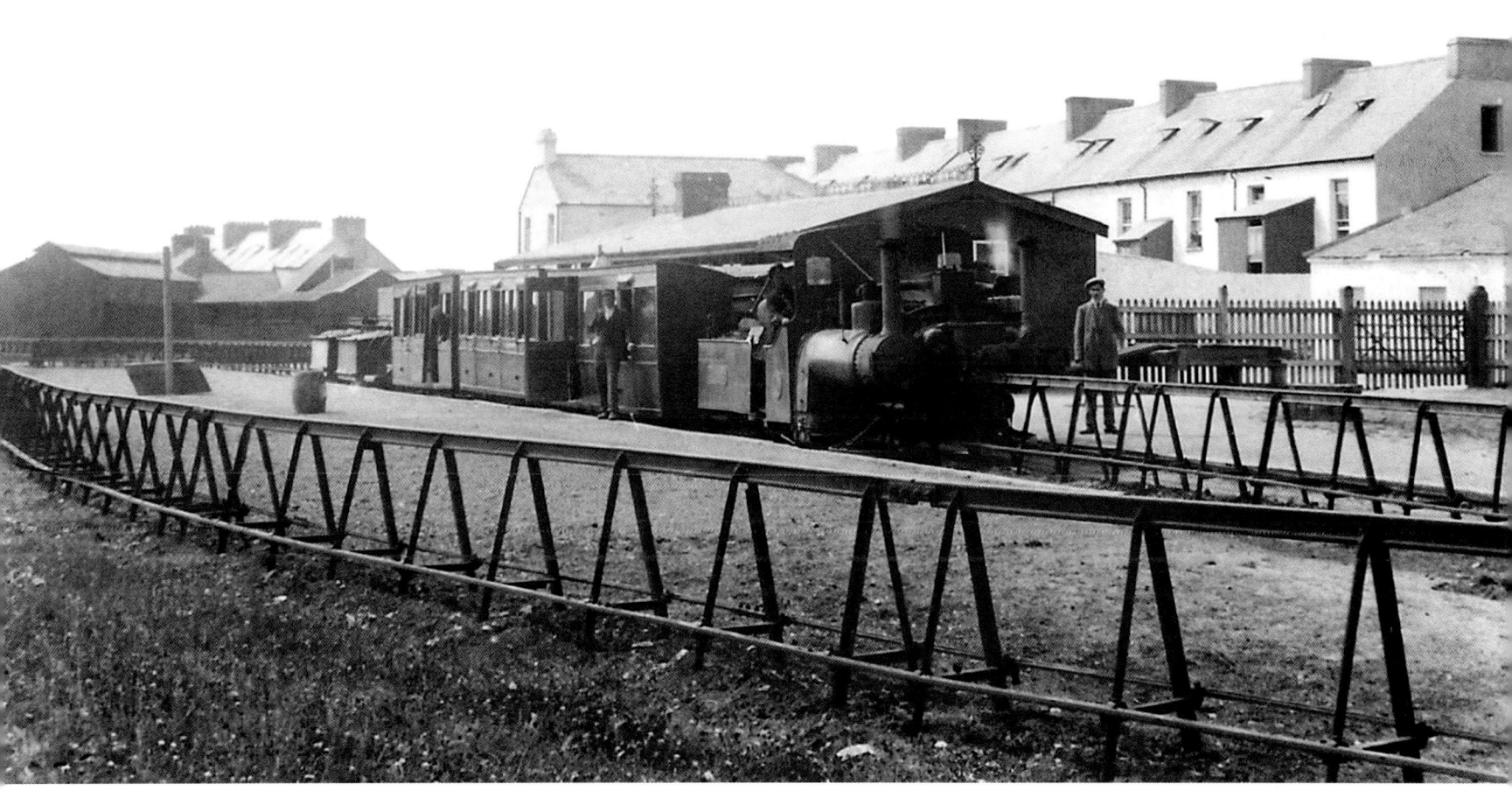

A second view of Ballybunion station showing 0-2-0 locomotive No.3 and a train of carriages in the station, waiting to depart to Listowel c.1900. If a cow needed to be transported along the line, it was necessary to have a second cow or goods in the other side of the wagon to balance the vehicle to run the train. The track was supported by A frames with outrigged guided rails. *Author's Collection*

A head on view of locomotive No.3 on the turntable at Ballybunion, showing the front end with its twin boilers and cylinder arrangement c.1920. *Author's Collection*

The Tralee & Dingle Railway was opened in March 1891, connecting the town of Tralee with Dingle on the Atlantic coast, serving a rural and fishing community. A large amount of cattle traffic was carried on the line and at one time some tourist traffic before the First World War. The railway became part of the Great Southern in 1925, with the passenger service being withdrawn in April 1939, along with all services on the Castle Gregory branch, after which the goods service continued until March 1947. However, cattle traffic continued on the line until April 1953 on a when-in-need basis, connected with the local cattle auctions. There is a short section of around a mile of railway preserved near Tralee which connects the Aquadrome with an historic windmill, using the last surviving T&D Hunslet 2-6-2 tank No.5 and a rake of imported bogie carriages. Hunslet constructed 2-6-0 tank No.3 and a mixed train stand in Tralee station, waiting to depart for Dingle c.1938. *Author's Collection*

Hunslet 2-6-0 tank locomotive No.3 constructed in 1889, stands outside the locomotive shed at Tralee c.1938; this picture shows the chunky bulk of these impressive powerful modern late nineteenth-century locomotives. *Author's Collection*

Hunslet 2-6-0 tank No.2 of 1889, on a mixed train of vans and passenger bogie carriages at Annascaul station c.1935. *Author's Collection*

The Dublin and Blessington steam tramway was constructed and promoted to link Dublin with Blessington. Opened in August 1888, the line was extended to Poulaphouca. Opening in 1885, this unusual steam tramway served the outer areas of Dublin, providing a regular passenger service for commuters and local people; here we see one of the 2-4-2 tram locomotives and two double deck bogie trailers at the Dublin terminus c.1920. After the First World War the tramway slowly declined as a result of road competition from bus services and finally closed, firstly from Blessington to Poulaphouca in November 1927 and lastly from Dublin to Blessington in December 1932. *Tom Middlemass Collection*

A second 2-4-2 tram locomotive waits at a wayside stop on the steam tramway, with its train of two double deck bogie tramcars, while its crew pose for the camera c.1910. The 2-4-2 tram locomotives were constructed by Thomas Green 1896 (two locomotives) and Brush (one locomotive) in 1899. *Hopwood Collection*

The Cavan & Leitrim Railway was opened in October 1887, linking the Great Northern Railway line at Belturbet with Dromod on the Midland & Great Western Railway; a branch later constructed to serve the colliery at Arigna opened in May 1888. The line served a mostly rural area, with passenger and goods services, also coal from the Arigna mine. Taken over by the Great Southern Railway in 1925 and CIÉ in 1945, the Cavan & Leitrim was finally closed to all traffic in February 1959. A general scene at Ballinamore station c.1930, showing the track layout and the goods yard. *Tom Middlemass Collection*

The Locomotive Works at Ballinamore with Robert Stephenson constructed 4-4-0 tank No.1 *Isobel* standing outside c.1927. It was here that all the heavy repairs to locomotives and rolling stock took place; later, in the 1930s, most of the locomotive heavy overhauls were carried out at Inchicore Works Dublin and this facility was slowly run down. *Tom Middlemass Collection*

Locomotive No.7 *Olive* at the head of a long-mixed train made up of a single balcony end bogie carriage a passenger brake van, open wagons and vans at Ballinamore station c.1924. The eight Robert Stephenson 4-4-0 tanks were constructed in 1887 for the opening of the line; they were named after the daughters of the original directors, except No.8 *Queen Victoria*, which lost its name during the Irish civil war around 1920, the names being removed after the Great Southern Railways take over in 1925. *Photomatic*

The Cavan & Leitrim received a number of batches of locomotives from other 3ft 0in gauge lines during the 1930s and 1940s. Among the newcomers to the line were the four former Cork & Blackrock Passage Railway 2-4-2 tanks, made redundant when that line closed in September 1932. Here we see No.10L on a service to Ballinamore waiting in the platform at Dromod, coupled to the bus coach, which was constructed by CIÉ during the 1950s to ascertain if such utilitarian vehicles could be used as replacements for older more conventional carriage stock August 1955. *Rev A.W.V. Mace*

The Cavan & Leitrim Railway had distinctive bogie carriage stock. Here we see a balcony end 1st 3rd carriage in Great Southern Railways days c.1938; note the original bodywork has been boarded over by this time, due to the carriage shed being demolished as a false economy and the stock being left out in all weathers, the elements taking its toll. *Tom Middlemass Collection*

The line also had three former Tralee & Dingle Hunslet tanks, two 2-6-0 and one 2-6-2. Here 2-6-0 tank No.3 constructed in 1889, simmers in the platform at Arigna station in August 1954, with a passenger service to Ballinamore. On the Cavan & Leitrim Railway they were referred to as Kerry men. No.5 the sole example of a Tralee & Dingle Railway 2-6-2 tank still exists and works on a heritage line near Tralee. *Rev A.W.V. Mace*

The County Donegal Railway has a complicated history. Its beginnings are that of an Irish standard 5ft 3in gauge line, the Finn Valley, from Strabane to Stranorlar, worked by the Irish North Western Railway until 1876 and thereafter by the Great Northern Railway of Ireland. The West Donegal Railway opened in 1882 from Stranorlar to Druminin and extended in September 1889 to Donegal and to Killybegs in July 1893, lastly to Glenties in July 1893. The Finn Valley Railway was converted to 3ft 0in gauge in July 1894, thus linking the 3ft 0in gauge network which formed the County Donegal Railway. The branch to Londonderry opened in August 1900, being followed finally by a line to Ballyshannon in September 1905, Henry Forbes being a leading light in the management and successful operation of the railway at this time. The railway was taken over by a joint committee managed by the English Midland Railway and the Great Northern Railway of Ireland in 1906, the LMS taking this role over in January 1923 and briefly British Railways in January 1948 for one year, before the Ulster Transport Authority and the Great Northern Railway of Ireland ran the committee. The network thrived until the 1920s when road competition started to deplete the railway's profits, after which branches started to be closed, firstly the line to Glenties in December 1947 and as the 1950s went on, other lines closed including the main line to Londonderry in 1954. The final curtain came down on the County Donegal Railway in December 1959, when the final trains ran and the company went over to road operation for goods and passengers. Today there are several museums along the route of the former railway that have important exhibits and relics from this once great concern, the best exhibits being in the Ulster Transport and Folk Museum at Cultra, near Belfast. Naismith Wilson 2-6-4 tank No.17 Glenties, constructed in 1907, with a passenger service entering Strabane station in June 1936. *Rev A.W.V. Mace*

Naismith Wilson 4-6-4 tank No.14 *Erne* stands in the platform at Stranorlar station c.1935, with a passenger service. This locomotive was the last surviving Baltic 4-6-4 tank in the British Isles and survived until the mid-1960s, when after cosmetic restoration it was cut up for scrap; today it would be a much loved and valued exhibit in a museum or working on a heritage line. *Author's Collection*

Twenty years later, a Walker railcar waits in the platform at Stranorlar, with a train consisting of the ex-Dublin & Blessington four wheeled trailer and a goods van c.1955. Walkers of Wigan supplied the County Donegal Railway with a number of diesel rail cars from the 1930s until the late 1940s, several examples of these CDR machines still exist in museum collections in Northern Ireland and on the Isle of Man. The County Donegal Railway was a pioneer in using rail cars to cut operating costs, having a fleet of various types from the late 1920s. *Author's Collection*

Four wheeled shunting locomotive No.11 *Phoenix* at Strabane c.1950. This locomotive started life as a steam locomotive constructed by Atkinson Walker in 1928, for the Clogher Valley Tramway, where it was unsuccessful, being sold to the CDR and converted into a diesel locomotive. This interesting locomotive is now part of the collection at the Ulster Transport and Folk Museum at Cultra, near Belfast. *Author's Collection*

The Londonderry & Lough Swilly Railway was another line that had a complicated history, starting life in November 1863 as a 5ft 3in railway constructed from Londonderry to Farland Point (closed in 1866) with a branch to Tooban Junction, with a connection to Buncrana for a steamer to Ramelton. The Latterkenny Railway opened in June 1883 from Cuttymanhill to Latterkenny, as a 3ft 0in line, worked by the L&LSR. The existing line was then converted from 5ft 3in to 3ft 0in gauge in 1885, extended from Buncrana to Carndonagh in July 1901 and from Latterkenny to Burtonport in March 1903, using a government grant. The section between Buncrana to Carndonagh closed in October 1935 and the section from Londonderry to Buncrana closed to passenger traffic in September 1948, closing completely in July 1953. In 1929, the L&LSR started to invest in road transport both goods and passenger with a fleet of Lorries and buses, operating services in the Londonderry area and the North West of Ireland. After running at a loss for some years, the bus company ceased trading in April 2014; by this time the company was the oldest transport operator still in existence established in Victorian times. Andrew Barclay-constructed locomotive No.2 of 1902 runs around its passenger train at Londonderry station May 1948. *F.A. Wycherley*

Hudswell Clarke 4-6-2 tank number 7 at Londonderry shed in C1935, this locomotive was originally named King Edward V11 when constructed in 1901, it was withdrawn from service in 1940. *Tom Middlemass Collection*

Andrew Barclay 4-6-0 tank No.1 arrives with a passenger service at Pennyburn station in August 1930. *Photomatic*

Hudswell Clarke 4-8-0 tender locomotive No.12, constructed in 1905, stands at Falcarragh station c.1935, with a mixed train to Burtonport on the Burtonport extension line. The Burtonport extension had its own locomotives and rolling stock, which were not meant to be used on the rest of the L&LSR. *Photomatic*

The Clogher Valley Railway (CVR) was opened in May 1887 as a steam tramway, connecting two main lines of the Great Northern Railway of Ireland at Maguire's Bridge on the Enniskillen to Clones line and Tynan on the Clones to Armagh line; it later changed its status to that of a railway in 1894. The tramway was a 3ft 0in gauge road side system, linking towns and villages in County Tyrone in Northern Ireland. During the late nineteenth century and until the First World War, the Railway prospered. However, after the war the line suffered from road competition, which resulted in its down fall, closing in December 1941. Sharp Stuart 0-4-2 tram locomotive No.6 *Erne,* constructed in 1887, waits in the platform at Maguiresbridge station c.1936, with a mixed train. *Tom Middlemass Collection*

Hudswell Clarke 2-6-2 tank No.4, constructed in 1904 for the Castlederg & Victoria Bridge Tramway and later sold to the CVR in 1936, by the contractor lifting the C&VB. The locomotive is seen here in the shed at Aughnacloy in June 1937, this premises was also the CVR works, where heavy repairs and overhauls were carried out on the locomotives and rolling stock. *Photomatic*

Walkers of Wigan supplied the tramway with this diesel rail car set in 1932 and also supplied a 0-4-0 diesel tractor a year later. Both these units were an attempt to offset the considerable losses the line made during its entire existence, here seen at Fivemiletown in June 1937.
Rev A.W.V. Mace

One of the attractive balcony end bogie carriages No.15 used on the line, here seen in c.1936. *Tom Middlemass Collection*

The Castlederg & Victoria Bridge Tramway was opened in July 1884, operating a line from Castlederg to Victoria Bridge, with passing loops at Spamount and Crew. The 3ft 0in gauge line had six steam locomotives including a Hudswell Clarke 0-4-4 tank No.5, also a Hudswell Clark 2-6-2 tank No.4 and a Beyer Peacock 2-4-0 tank purchased from the Ballymena & Larne Railway No.6. The line suffered from road competition and was also in need of heavy repairs by the early 1930s and after a railway strike in 1932, it was decided to close the line and lift the track. Here we see the former Ballymena & Larne 2-4-0 tank after the lines closure in January 1933, in use by the contractor on demolition trains.
Author's Collection

The Fintona Horse Tram operated on the branch line from Fintona town to Fintona Junction, on the Londonderry to Enniskillen main line of the Great Northern Railway of Ireland opened in June 1883. The line to Fintona became a branch when the main line to Londonderry bypassed the town in 1856, after which there was a need to connect the town with the junction. This was done using a road coach on flanged wheels and later this was replaced with a double deck horse tram, which was used on the branch until 1 October 1957, when the main line and the Fintona branch closed. The horse was always called Dick even when the horse was a mare and was housed in a timber shed between turns in case the horse was frightened by passing trains. The horse tram is now preserved in the Ulster Transport and Folk Museum at Cultra near Belfast, the picture depicts the tram at Fintona in 1931. *Local Postcard*

The Ballycastle Railway was opened to traffic in October 1880, originally operated by the Belfast & Northern Counties Railway; the line was taken over by the English Midland Railway in 1903 and grouped into the LMS in 1923, becoming the LMS Northern Counties Committee. In 1948 the system became part of British Railways London Midland Region for a year before being handed over to the Ulster Transport Authority in 1949, who closed the line in July 1950. 0-6-0 tank locomotive No.106 waits in Ballycastle station with a short train of two bogie carriages in August 1930, waiting the off for its journey to Ballymoney. *Photomatic*

0-6-0 tank locomotive No.106 at Ballycastle station c.1930, while shunting goods wagons in the station yard. *Author's Collection*

The Ballymena & Larne Railway was opened in August 1877 operating a line from Retreat near Red Bay to the harbour at Larne via Ballymena, where it connected to the main line to Belfast on the B&NCR; the railway was taken over by the Belfast & Northern Counties Railway in 1889 and the English Midland Railway in 1903 and grouped into the LMS in 1923, becoming part of the LMSNCC, taken into the London Midland Region of British Railways in 1948, being handed over to the Ulster Transport Authority in 1949, who closed the line in July 1950. Beyer Peacock 2-6-0 Saddle Tank No.109 simmers in the station at Ballyboley with a local passenger service c.1930. *Photomatic*

Bayer Peacock compound 2-4-2 tank No.102 departs Ballymena with a local passenger train in August 1930, these 2-4-2 tanks were very powerful for their size and worked the boat trains to Larne harbour. *Photomatic*

The 3ft 0in gauge Portstewart Tramway was opened in June 1882, connecting Portstewart station to Portstewart Town, a distance of 1.85 Miles, it was taken over by the Belfast & Northern Counties Railway in 1897 and the English Midland Railway in 1903, becoming part of the LMSNCC at grouping in 1923. The line did not make a profit, so it was decided to close the tramway in 1926. Two of the three Kitson constructed 0-4-0 tram locomotives are preserved, No.1 of 1882 in the transport museum in Hull and No.2 of 1883 in the Ulster Transport & Folk Museum in Cultra, near Belfast, the third of 1901, was sold to the contractor lifting the tramway in 1926. One of the Kitson tram locomotives waits at Portstewart railway station c.1910. *Hopwood Collection*

Giants Causeway has long been a tourist attraction, so therefore it was logical to construct a tramway to take visitors to this world famous attraction. The tramway opened in January 1883 as a steam operated line, with 0-4-0 vertical boiler tram locomotives constructed by Wilkinson and a fleet of four wheeled tram carriages, some open and some with basic roofs with open sides. The picture shows a tram locomotive with three trailers c.1898. Steam was withdrawn from the tramway in 1899. *Author's Collection*

The tramway was later electrified with a conductor rail in 1887 and later in 1899 with overhead wire pick up, seen here in c.1930. The tramway was finally closed completely in 1949. *Author's Collection*

The Isle of Man

The Isle of Man once had an extensive 3ft 0in gauge railway network serving most of the island, The first stage of the system opened in July 1874 from Douglas to Peel and the second section from Douglas to Port Erin opened in August 1874. The Manx Northern was opened in September 1879 and was taken over by the Isle of Man Railway (IOMR) in February 1904, at the same time as the IOMR took over the Foxdale branch. After many years of loss making and bus competition, the IOMR was gradually closed down until today there is only a modest section of the former system left between Douglas and Port Erin, which runs during the summer months. Beyer Peacock 2-4-0 tank No.2 *Derby*, constructed in 1873, leaves Douglas with a passenger service c.1950.
Tom Middlemass Collection

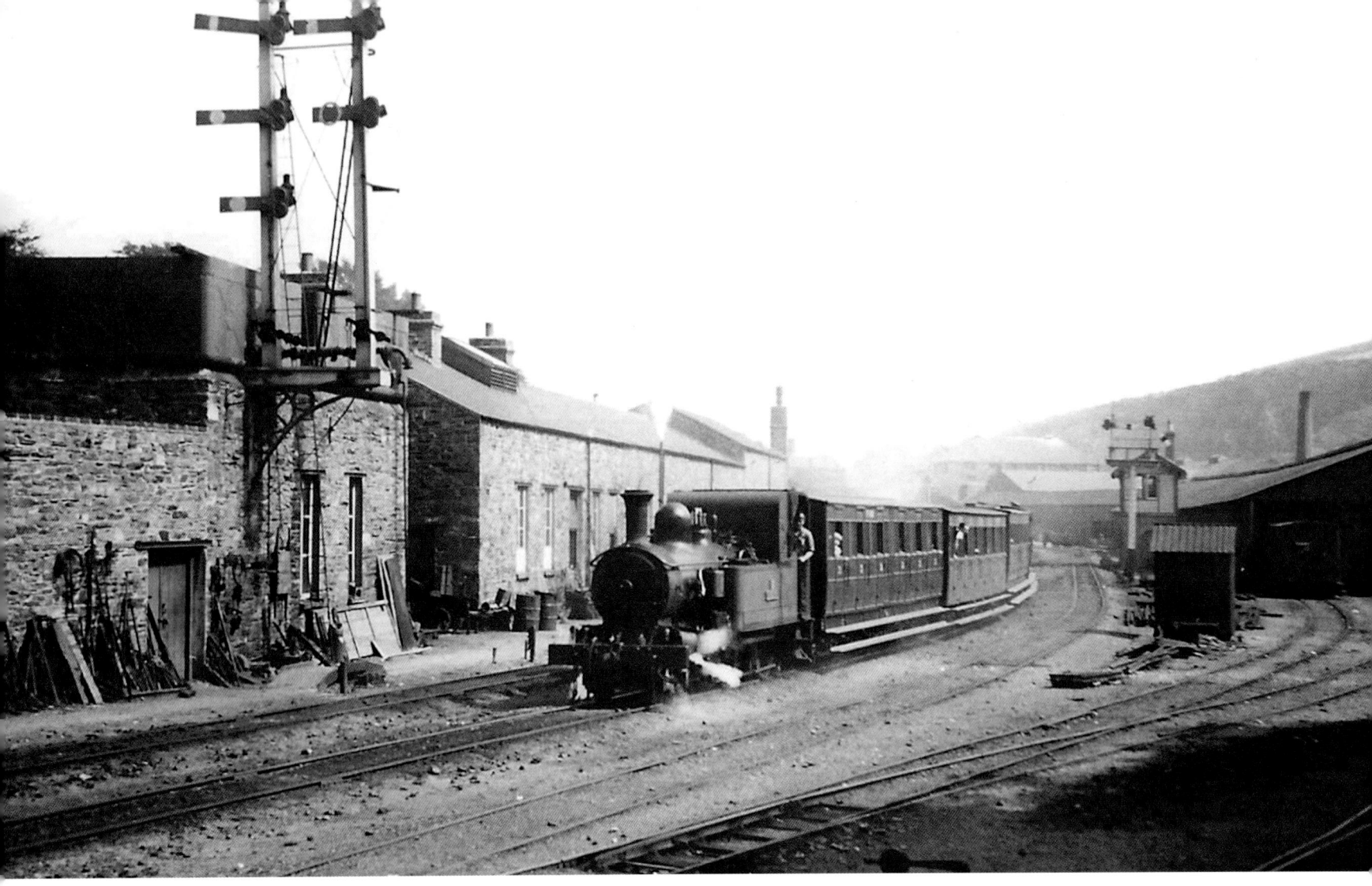

A Beyer Peacock 2-4-0 tank steams through the outskirts of Douglas with a passenger train c.1949. *Tom Middlemass Collection*

Locomotive No.1 *Sutherland*, constructed by Beyer Peacock in 1873, with its crew posing for the camera c.1920. *Tom Middlemass Collection*

Locomotive No.16 *Mannin* in pristine condition shortly after delivery. This was the final Beyer Peacock 2-4-0 tank constructed for the IOMR in 1926. *Tom Middlemass Collection*

The Groudle Glen Railway

This short pleasure 2ft 0in gauge line was opened in 1895 by Groudle Ltd to transport tourists from Groudle Glen to the Sea Lion Rocks and Zoo, which housed polar bears and sealions. The railway was very popular with our Victorian ancestors and continued to be so until the First World War, when the line closed for the duration and the zoo was closed for good. The line reopened in the post war era and the two W.G. Bagnall 2-4-0 tanks returned after overhauls to resume their duties. Also during this time the railway introduced two battery 2-4-2 locomotives, which were only moderately successful in service. The line closed again for the duration of the Second World War, reopening after the end of hostilities in the late 1940. Due to losses incurred during the 1950s and early 1960s, when fewer people visited the Glen, the railway closed in 1962 and was left derelict for some time.

Both steam locomotives were sold to preservation groups, *Polar Bear* going to the Narrow Gauge Railway Society, who established a base at Brockham in Surrey and later Amberley Chalk Pits Museum in West Sussex, the second locomotive *Sea Lion* stayed on the Island and is now part of the revived Groudle Glen Railway, which is run by volunteers, who have restored the full length of the railway.

W.G. Bagnall 2-4-0 tank locomotive *Polar Bear* constructed in 1898, here seen in c.1930, this locomotive is now preserved at the Chalk Pits Museum at Amberley West Sussex. *Author's Collection*

One of the 2-4-2 battery locomotives constructed by British Electric Vehicles Ltd, on a train at the terminus station at Groudle Glen c.1925. These locomotives were not a great success and steam traction was soon back hauling the trains of holiday visitors. *Local Postcard*